R.F.K.

OTHER BOOKS BY DICK SCHAAP

MICKEY MANTLE
PAUL HORNUNG
AN ILLUSTRATED HISTORY OF THE OLYMPICS
TURNED ON

R.F.K.

BY DICK SCHAAP

PICTURE EDITOR: MICHAEL O'KEEFE

THE NEW AMERICAN LIBRARY

First Printing

Published by The New American Library, Inc.
1301 Avenue of the Americas, New York, New York 10019
Published simultaneously in Canada by
General Publishing Company, Ltd.

Library of Congress Catalog Card Number: 67-28481

Printed in the United States of America

Designed by Ony Ryzuk

CONTENTS

AUTHOR'S NOTE AND ACKNOWLEDGMENTS

This biography was neither authorized nor approved, and it must be recorded that its subject, Senator Robert Francis Kennedy, who was cooperative without being enthusiastic about the project, made only one request of the author. The first time we met after the research began, I mentioned that I had read considerable background material and I had, at the start, only one pressing question: Was his wife, Ethel, really as good a touch-football player as some accounts claimed?

"Would you do me one favor?" said Senator Kennedy. "Would you point out that my wife can do other things besides play sports?"

A cynical friend, when he heard the senator's request, said, "See, he wants you to lie already."

The senator's request, I hope, has been filled—truthfully.

This book is intended as an objective study of a man who inspires subjectivity much more readily than objectivity. Yet I am as grateful for the subjective views as for the factual material provided to me by many sources, by Robert Kennedy's friends and Robert Kennedy's enemies. All of Senator Kennedy's staff was helpful, especially the press secretary, Frank Mankiewicz, and his assistant, Patricia Riley. I appreciate the time and the information offered by men who once worked with Senator Kennedy—including Ed Guthman, John Seigenthaler, Daniel Patrick Moynihan, and Lawrence O'Brien—and the aid of many journalists, most notably Benjamin Bradlee and Andrew Glass of *The Washington Post,* Bob Healy of *The Boston Globe*, and George Tames and Richard Reeves of *The New York Times*, and Marty Nolan of *The Reporter* Magazine.

Many books were invaluable, particularly Nick Thimmesch and William Johnson's *Robert Kennedy at 40*, Hugh Sidey's chapter on Robert Kennedy in *The Kennedy Circle*, Pierre Salinger's *With Kennedy*, Arthur Schlesinger Jr.'s *A Thousand Days*, William Manchester's *The Death of a President*, and Theodore White's 1960 and 1964 accounts of *The Making of the President*.

I must express special thanks to Lucille Beachy of *Newsweek* magazine, who gathered research material for this book, and to my editor, Robert A. Gutwillig, who provided guidance, encouragement, and, like everyone else, his own share of subjectivity.

R.F.K.

CHAPTER ONE

THE TURNING POINT

At 1:30 p.m. Eastern Standard Time, Friday, November 22, 1963, Robert Francis Kennedy, refreshed after a quick prelunch swim, casually dressed in sports shirt and shorts, sat by the pool behind his Virginia home and sipped New England clam chowder. At precisely the same time, in the black sunlight of Dallas, the first bullet struck his brother.

He would willingly have taken the bullet himself.

Already, he had submerged his own ambitions and his own causes in his brother's. Often he had thrown himself in front of verbal assaults upon his brother, sometimes deflecting them, sometimes absorbing them, apparently relishing his role as a substitute target. But on the day that John Fitzgerald Kennedy died, on the day that his own life suddenly veered off course, Robert Kennedy, the Attorney General of the United States, was 1,300 miles from the President, half a continent removed from Lee Harvey Oswald's line of fire.

Early Wednesday evening, November 20, at a White House reception for the members of the Supreme Court, Bobby Kennedy had seen John Kennedy alive for the final time. Then the Attorney General had hurried home to Hickory Hill, his sprawling estate in McLean, Virginia, to a party celebrating his own thirty-eighth birthday. His brother had not attended the party. His brother had needed some rest before he left the next morning for Texas.

A few seconds after the first shot, another bullet ripped into John F. Kennedy and tore away the top of his head. By 1:40 p.m. E.S.T., millions of Americans knew, if little more, that someone in Texas had shot at the President of the United States.

Bobby Kennedy knew nothing. He sat by his swimming pool, nibbling a tuna-fish sandwich. He sat with his wife, Ethel, and with two guests, Robert Morgenthau, the United States Attorney in New York, and Silvio Mollo, Morgenthau's chief assistant. From his seat by the pool, Bob Morgenthau could see a workman hanging shutters on a new wing of the Kennedys' white brick house. The workman was listening to a transistor radio.

Los Angeles, 1960. The Democratic National Convention. "Already, he had submerged his own ambitions and his own causes in his brother's."

Suddenly, the workman deserted the shutters and hurried across the lawn to the foursome gathered by the swimming pool. "It says on the radio . . .," he began, and then he faltered and his words came out garbled. On the opposite side of the shallow end of the swimming pool, a special telephone, White House extension 163, began ringing.

Bobby Kennedy glanced at his watch. The time was 1:45 p.m. While the workman struggled to make himself understood, Ethel Kennedy walked to the phone and lifted the white receiver. "It's J. Edgar Hoover," she called to her husband.

The Attorney General dropped his sandwich and ran to the telephone. "I have news for you," Hoover said. "The President's been shot."

Simultaneously, the workman managed to repeat what he had heard on his transistor radio to Morgenthau, Mollo, and Ethel Kennedy.

"I think it's serious," Hoover said. "I am endeavoring to get details. I'll call you back when I find out more."

Bobby Kennedy hung up, slapped his hand over his mouth and for ten, perhaps fifteen, seconds turned away from his guests. He stared at nothing. Then he turned back. "The President was shot," he said.

Ethel Kennedy rushed to her husband and embraced him, and his face filled with horror, but he did not break, he did not cry. Immediately, he decided to fly to Dallas to join his brother. He returned to the telephone, called Robert Mc-Namara, and asked the Secretary of Defense to arrange transportation. Then he sprinted inside to change his clothes.

Morgenthau and Mollo retreated tactfully to a study where they could watch television. Soon, they were joined by a neighbor, Sue Markham, the wife of Dean

The pictures on these pages were taken at Hickory Hill, Robert and Ethel Kennedy's home in McLean, Virginia, several months before the assassination of President Kennedy.

R. F. K.

Markham, once Bobby Kennedy's Harvard football teammate and, in 1963, executive director of the United States Narcotics Commission. They heard only fragmented, confused news bulletins. They did not know that John F. Kennedy lay dying on a table in Parkland Memorial Hospital's Trauma Room No. 1.

In Washington, the President's youngest brother, Senator Edward Kennedy, who, ironically, had been sitting in for Lyndon Johnson as the presiding officer of the Senate when the fatal shot was fired, searched frantically for a working telephone. The lines in the capital were terribly overloaded.

Upstairs at Hickory Hill, Bobby Kennedy clung to the phone as he changed his clothes. From the White House, Captain Tazewell Shepard, the President's naval aide, offered to help inform members of the family. From Dallas, Clint Hill of the Secret Service relayed details of the shooting and of the wound. "What kind of doctors do they have?" the Attorney General asked. "How is Jackie taking it?"

As he switched from extension to extension, Bobby Kennedy, thinking of Dallas, grumbled aloud, "There's been so much hate." He talked to McNamara again, and he talked to John McCone, the director of the Central Intelligence Agency, and while he talked, at 2 p.m. E.S.T., Dr. William Kemp Clark, the chief neurosurgeon at Parkland Memorial Hospital, pronounced the President dead.

And still Bobby Kennedy changed his clothes, hoping to see his brother alive. John McCone reached Hickory Hill and climbed to the upstairs library. "Do you know how serious the wound is?" McCone asked.

"No," said the Attorney General, "I don't." He straightened his tie and adjusted his tie pin, a gold miniature of PT-109, the boat his brother had skippered during World War II.

Then, at 2:05 p.m., the White House extension rang on his desk. He picked up the phone, heard Captain Shepard's report, and winced. "Oh," said Bobby Kennedy softly, "he's dead."

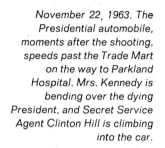

Two of Robert Kennedy's sons share their father's sorrow shortly after learning that the President has died.

Ethel Kennedy, standing nearby, began to cry. "Those poor children," she said. "He had the most wonderful life," said her husband.

Quietly the Kennedys and McCone descended the staircase. In the study a television announcer mouthed a vaguely optimistic report. Bobby Kennedy looked into the study. "He's dead," he said.

Quickly the crowd began to gather, the friends and the associates, drawn to Hickory Hill to comfort the Kennedys and to comfort themselves. They came shaken and sad, bitter and lost, and they drew most of their comfort from Bobby Kennedy. He functioned. "We don't want any gloomy faces around here," he told Dave Hackett, a friend since childhood. Kennedy considered flying to Dallas to accompany the President's body home, then dismissed the idea; he dispatched his surviving brother to Hyannis Port to tell their ailing father that the President was dead; he began setting the funeral plans in motion. In action and in fact, he took command of the Kennedy family.

And in Texas, Lyndon Johnson took command of the country. At 3 p.m. E.S.T., White House extension 163 rang by the pool once more. The call came from Love Field in Dallas, from Air Force One, the Presidential jet, from Lyndon Baines Johnson. The new President offered his condolences, mentioned his suspicion of "a worldwide plot," then asked the Attorney General's advice. "A lot of people down here think I should be sworn in right away," said Lyndon Johnson. "Do you have any objection to that?"

Kennedy hesitated, saying nothing.

R. F. K.

"Congressman Albert Thomas thinks I should take the oath here," Johnson said. "A lot of other people feel the same way."

Still the Attorney General remained silent.

"Who could swear me in?" Johnson asked.

"I'll be glad to find out and call you back," said Kennedy.

The Attorney General telephoned his chief deputy, Nicholas Katzenbach. "Lyndon wants to be sworn in in Texas," Kennedy said, "and wants to know who can administer the oath."

Katzenbach checked with an aide, confirmed his own feeling that anyone could administer the Presidental oath who regularly administered oaths under federal or state laws, then repeated the information to the Attorney General. Kennedy relayed the report to Dallas, and at 3:38 p.m. E.S.T., aboard Air Force One, Lyndon Baines Johnson was sworn in as the thirty-sixth President of the United States.

The thousand days of John Fitzgerald Kennedy had ended.

The life Robert Francis Kennedy had known had ended too.

His own grief would come later, in months of indecision, as he drifted preoccupied through a world stripped of its most familiar landmark, but on the day of the assassination, and in the days that followed, Bobby Kennedy did everything he had to do; he did more than anyone could have expected. He suffered

Jacqueline Kennedy holds Caroline's hand as Chief Justice Earl Warren eulogizes President Kennedy in the Capitol rotunda. Left to right: Stephen Smith, President Lyndon Johnson, Eunice Kennedy Shriver, Robert Kennedy, Peter Lawford (comforting daughter), Patricia Kennedy Lawford, Jean Kennedy Smith, Ethel Kennedy. (opposite page) Jacqueline and Caroline Kennedy touch and kiss the flag draped across the President's casket.

through the awful arrival of the body at Andrews Air Force Base, hiding in the rear of a truck until Air Force One touched down, then racing aboard in the darkness so that he could escort his brother's widow from the plane. He kept himself stiffly controlled through the memorial service, through the eulogies, through the funeral.

12

(opposite and right) The Kennedy family, and President and Mrs. Johnson leave the Capitol after the eulogies. (below) November 25. Robert, Jacqueline, and Edward Kennedy walking down the steps of the Capitol after visiting the President's casket before the funeral mass at St. Matthew's Cathedral.

Yet Lee Harvey Oswald's bullets had pierced the brother too.

Until the assassination, Bobby Kennedy had given his own future no more than a glancing thought. "He never really thought about a next job," Ed Guthman, the Attorney General's press secretary, said later. "He figured the next job would take care of itself." His only job, past, present, and future, was to help his brother.

"It's all right, I'm not running for anything," Bobby Kennedy would say when he bore the attacks aimed at his brother. "I'm never going to be running for anything."

But now, abruptly, Lyndon Johnson was President.

And now, without warning, Bobby Kennedy had no brother to defend, no brother to promote.

R. F. K.

15

(left) Jacqueline Kennedy, flanked by the President's brothers, completes the walk from the White House to St. Matthew's Cathedral behind the casket of the President. (below) After the funeral mass, the President's casket is carried from the church to the caisson. (opposite page) — Above, the famous picture of John F. Kennedy, Jr. saluting his father's casket as it is placed on the caisson outside St. Matthew's. Below — a picture taken moments later — John, still trying to salute, wipes the tears from his eyes.

17

And now, for the first time in years, perhaps for the first time in his life, Bobby Kennedy had to consider seriously his own career. His brother's death triggered questions he could not ignore:

Did he want to stay in public life?

Did he want to work with President Lyndon Johnson?

Did he want to run for elective office?

And, ultimately, during the agonizing months of decisions made and decisions thrust upon him, even as he lost his chance for the Vice Presidency in 1964 and he won his seat in the United States Senate, he had to face the major question, a question that had been raised before, but often as a joke:

Did Robert Francis Kennedy want to become President of the United States?

Of course he did.

19

CHAPTER TWO
A DAY WITH R.F.K.

He came to the long dining room table wrapped in a monogrammed blue robe, and his wife greeted him, "Hail, Caesar." His blue eyes bleary from lack of sleep, his face unshaven, his hair even more unruly than usual, he seated himself to a breakfast of poached eggs and bacon, lifting the bacon with his fingers, and his hands began to quiver, slightly but noticeably. It may have been only fatigue, or it may have been the one overt sign of nervousness Robert F. Kennedy permitted himself on March 2, 1967, the day he delivered to the United States Senate his proposals to bring peace to Vietnam.

Nervousness was logical. More than three years had elapsed since the death of his brother, since he had been forced to set off on his own course, and now he was a senator. He was only the junior senator from New York, yet when he spoke his voice carried weight far beyond his title, beyond his experience, beyond the words themselves. His voice carried the weight of his name, the weight of his brother's memory.

His speech on Vietnam had been trumpeted and anticipated for weeks, a speech that would be interpreted by many as a decisive break with Lyndon Johnson, that would be cited by many as further proof of Bobby Kennedy's political impatience and imprudence, that would displease all of the hawks, all who urged an expansion of American war efforts in Vietnam, and some of the doves, those who viewed with distrust any speech tempered by political discretion, those who sought little short of an immediate American withdrawal from Vietnam.

Bobby Kennedy knew his speech was certain to provoke strong political emotions, certain to inspire official retaliation, perhaps massive, perhaps Machiavellian. He turned to his wife, Ethel, who sat at his side, smiling, incorrigibly cheerful, dressed in her customary fashion, a purple maternity dress; she was expecting her tenth child in a few weeks. "I spoke to Teddy last night," the senator told his wife. "He said to make sure that they announce it's the Kennedy from New York."

THE WHITE HOUSE
WASHINGTON

July 12, 1935.

Dear Bob:-

Your Dad has told me that you are a
stamp collector and I thought you might like
to have these stamps to add to your collection.
I am also enclosing a little album which you
may find useful.

Perhaps sometime when you are in
Washington you will come in and let me show
you my collection.

My best wishes to you,

Very sincerely yours,

Robert Kennedy,
Hyannisport,
Massachusetts.

(Enclosure)

*President Roosevelt's letter to
then ten-year-old Bob Kennedy
hangs just inside the front
door at Hickory Hill.*

Kennedy grinned drowsily, pleased with his small joke. He delights in, and excels at, poking sly fun at himself; it is, quite likely, his most human, most winning characteristic. "A lot of people think I'm out of my mind," he said. "You could almost get a unanimous opinion on that."

This would be, before it ended, a day of chaos and of machinations, a day demanding and exposing all the elements of the Kennedy style, a day of wit and intelligence, of open ambition and veiled bitterness. The day would be almost a miniature of Robert Kennedy's life as a senator, with overtones from his past and hints of his future.

But now, as Bobby Kennedy ate breakfast, Hickory Hill seemed strangely quiet, briefly peaceful. Somewhere upstairs in the vast 150-year-old house, Richard Goodwin, former speechwriter for John F. Kennedy (his "Alliance for Progress" speech) and Lyndon B. Johnson (his "Great Society" speech), presently Senior Fellow at Wesleyan University's Center for Advanced Studies, labored over a portable typewriter, carried to him shortly after 8 a.m. by one of the Kennedys' maids. "Poor Mr. Goodwin," she said. "He's been up all night."

"Who's Mr. Good*man*?" demanded three-year-old Christopher Kennedy, not visibly impressed.

It had been a long night—for Goodwin, for Bobby Kennedy, and for three others, Adam Walinsky, one of Kennedy's legislative aides; Frank Mankiewicz, Kennedy's press secretary; and Angela Novello, Kennedy's personal secretary. (The four men, incidentally, were all nonpracticing lawyers.) They had gathered at 9 p.m., huddled in the kitchen while a fire blazed in the den, and they had started with a draft of the Vietnam speech, and they had reworked it from beginning to end, shifting paragraphs, junking whole pages, inserting timely points. "Let's change that," Bobby Kennedy sometimes said. Or: "I don't want to say that."

Kennedy himself escaped to his bed from 3:30 a.m. to 7, but he slept little. Angie Novello, typing the new draft, did not sleep at all. Goodwin, too, worked through the night, and Walinsky stayed until 6 a.m., then went home to sleep for a few hours and reached the office on Capitol Hill shortly after 10 a.m. Mankiewicz left Hickory Hill for his home at 3:30 a.m., returned two hours later, expecting to pick up the speech and deliver it to secretaries who had been instructed to come to the office at 6 a.m. The speech was not ready until 7:45; Mankiewicz called the office and told the girls to go out for breakfast.

Between 7:45 and 8:30 a.m., while maids shuttled trays of eggs and coffee upstairs and downstairs, Bobby Kennedy's children ruled Hickory Hill. The almost final version of a major foreign-policy address had just been hammered out in the throbbing fifteen-room house that was once the Virginia headquarters of the Union forces, and now, judging by the noise, the army had returned.

Right in the main hallway, Bobby Jr., twelve years old; David, eleven; and Michael, eight, staged a rousing soccer session with a basketball. Kicking and shouting, they charged past the glass-framed historical documents lining the hall. Just inside the front door—a door bearing the legend, "*Chien Mechant*" (Beware of the Dog)—hung a letter written in 1935 by Franklin Delano Roosevelt. The President of the United States wrote the letter to a ten-year-old boy named Robert Kennedy. President Roosevelt told Bobby that they shared an interest in stamps and that the next time he journeyed to Washington with his father he should stop at the White House and inspect the F.D.R. collection.

In a den near the front door, Christopher and Matthew Maxwell Taylor Kennedy, two years old, struggled for possession of yellow, red, and pink balloons left over from a recent party. Brumus, a lumbering Newfoundland, the giant of the Kennedy kennel, joined the struggle; two other dogs, Battle Star and Freckles, lounged around the room. On the crowded wall hung a photograph of John Kennedy with Bobby Jr., young Bobby thoughtfully pressing his thumb against his lip. His uncle had captioned the photo: "A President gets his advice from many sources."

Kerry Kennedy, seven years old, lay upstairs nursing a cold; Kathleen, fifteen, and Joseph, fourteen, were away at boarding schools. Of all the Kennedy children, only Courtney, nine, quietly collecting her notebooks, seemed even remotely aware of the significance of the day.

Certainly Robert Kennedy himself did not bring to the morning the bright exuberance of his children. "I know more than they do," he explained.

Since the start of 1967, Bobby Kennedy had been weighing seriously the advisability of a major dissenting speech on Vietnam. The New Left and the Old Left, the academic community and the intellectual community, pressed him to speak out; so did many of his staff members and friends. (A few urged him to remain discreetly silent.) His conscience prodded him; so did his political instincts. In February, 1966, he had issued a major statement on Vietnam, a statement most

" 'I loved the Monday speech,' offered Ethel Kennedy, beaming."

"The almost final version of a major foreign-policy address had just been hammered out in the throbbing fifteen-room house that was once the Virginia headquarters of the Union forces and now, judging by the noise, the army had returned."

notable for its support of a post-truce coalition government, including the Viet Cong, in South Vietnam. Kennedy had retreated a few steps after the speech, insisting that he had meant only considering including the Viet Cong, not automatically including them, but clearly, as in earlier speeches on nuclear proliferation and in later ones on Red China, he had carved out his own political niche to the left of President Johnson and, just as important, to the left of Vice President Humphrey.

For a year after his coalition speech, Kennedy skirted the subject of Vietnam, but when he traveled to Europe at the end of January, 1967, his discussions with Prime Minister Wilson, President de Gaulle, Chancellor Kiesinger, Foreign Ministers Brown, Couve de Murville, Brandt, and Fanfani, and Pope Paul fed him ideas and information. His desire to speak out grew stronger.

He returned to Washington for a bitter confrontation with the President on February 6, in which Kennedy indicated both his urge to speak and his ideas, and the President warned him, in harsh words, that he would practically be betraying the troops in Vietnam. The meeting could scarcely have been less harmonious. Kennedy and his staff leaked details demonstrating how obdurate, how unreasonable the President had been; Lyndon Johnson and his staff countered with details demonstrating how tactless, how insulting the senator had been.

After the mutually frustrating session, Kennedy consulted officials at the United Nations and, from their comments, gained confidence that his plan was, at least, possible. He dipped into textbooks for facts bolstering his position, and he even questioned, in his New York apartment, Staughton Lynd and Tom Hayden, two voices of the New Left who had ignored government restrictions and visited Hanoi.

As the ideological and tactical pressures for his speech multiplied, Kennedy debated his timing. He reached his final decision while perched precariously— an omen, perhaps—on the edge of his bathtub. In mid-February, enjoying the luxury of bathroom TV, he heard Premier Kosygin, speaking from London via satellite, indicate that a halt in the American bombing of North Vietnam could lead to negotiations. "It was so clear to me," Kennedy said later, "that it didn't make any sense to go on bombing after Kosygin made his statement."

Immediately, he began plotting his speech. Dick Goodwin, the chief non-staff speechwriter, quickly worked up one draft; Adam Walinsky, the chief staff speechwriter, worked up another. Kennedy sought the advice of Arthur Schlesinger Jr., the historian who had served his brother, and Schlesinger responded with written suggestions. Theodore Sorensen, once special counsel to John F. Kennedy, read one draft, edited it, and returned it to Kennedy. Perhaps half a dozen others offered ideas.

"All the people basically agreed," said Kennedy. "They just differed on the specifics."

Kennedy himself, of course, supervised the merging of the two drafts with the fringe contributions. Typically, he had briefed Goodwin and Walinsky independently on what he wanted to say, what he wanted to stress, and, armed with their products—Walinsky's more radical than Goodwin's—he superimposed his own phrases, his own point of view. He listened, too, to recommendations from Frank Mankiewicz and Joseph Dolan, his administrative assistant. Dolan, no speechwriter himself, provided, as usual, candid criticisms; in the margin of one draft, he wrote, for instance, "Stand up and talk. Don't apologize." The changes affected tone more than content—how severely to criticize the recent escalation, how strongly to praise Lyndon Johnson as a man of peace, how much to emphasize the impossibility of military victory.

By design and by accident, bits of the speech's scope and substance leaked out; favored columnists and reporters floated trial balloons, calculated to build an atmosphere of expectation and drama, focusing national attention on the speech. The Kennedy team orchestrated the speech heavily, so heavily that some people began to suspect that the speech itself had to be anticlimactic. The leaks inspired premature rebuttal; the week before Kennedy's speech, James A. Farley, the former Postmaster General and Democratic National Chairman, condemned Kennedy's "soaring ambitions" and warned, "Insulting, belittling, and interfering with the office of the Presidency is not the act of a mature citizen, let

alone a United States senator." Neither the tone nor the thrust of his talk, Farley said afterward, had been suggested to him by anyone in the Johnson Administration. He did, however, mail a copy of his text to Lyndon Johnson.

Delicately, even as the preliminary attacks and defenses began, the speech was drafted and redrafted, and, although the core was firm more than a week before delivery, the exact language shifted from day to day. Finally, on Thursday, March 2, 1967, after three days of postponements, Bobby Kennedy was ready to present his proposals.

"I wonder what I would have done," he said, over breakfast at Hickory Hill, "if I'd had to deliver the speech Monday the way I'd planned."

"I loved the Monday speech," offered Ethel Kennedy, beaming.

Now Kennedy pushed himself away from the table and started upstairs, to shave, to dress, to polish his speech once more, and his wife led two visiting newspapermen to the basement to show them a few of the pets assembled by Robert F. Kennedy Jr. He collects pets the way his father collects opinions.

Ethel Kennedy opened the door gingerly to the room housing young Bobby's animal kingdom. "His newest," she said, "is a coati mundi. You should see him jump. He leaped over a couch chasing Bobby."

The coati mundi, a long, low, raccoon-like animal with a protruding, flexible snout, sharp claws, and prominent teeth, greeted the safari. At first, the native was friendly. He began climbing over one of the newspapermen, pawing gently at his pants leg.

Ethel Kennedy turned and moved toward Bobby's reptile cage, the home of his iguanas and snakes. Suddenly she screamed. Then she screamed again.

"Get him off me," she cried. "Get him off me. He's biting me. Oh, God, he's biting me." The coati mundi had attacked from the side, digging his claws and teeth into her unprotected legs, and now, heavy with pregnancy, Ethel Kennedy shook herself violently, the animal clinging to her, biting her, scratching her.

One of the newspapermen lifted the senator's wife off the floor and atop a wooden cabinet and, when the coati mundi let go, kicked the pet across the room. The other newspaperman opened the door, let the animal out into the hall, slammed the door, then rushed out a back door and ran to the front of the house to warn everyone that a coati mundi was dashing around loose.

Ethel Kennedy sat on the edge of the cabinet, trembling, pale, pained, her legs reddened by scratches and blood. "I'm so sorry," she kept saying to the newspaperman with her. "I'm so sorry."

Then a friend, Sue Markham, entered through the back door, and all of a sudden, as if by conditioned reflex, Ethel Kennedy composed herself. Properly, almost formally, she introduced Sue Markham to the visitor, the visitor to Sue Markham. And then, after her perfect display of Kennedy grace under pressure, Ethel began shaking again, her breath coming convulsively.

Upstairs, her husband still worked with Goodwin on his speech. Occasionally, either Kennedy or Goodwin would phone the senator's office and dictate a change to Mankiewicz or Walinsky or Peter Edelman, another legislative aide. The change would be commented upon and noted and passed to a secretary who would re-type the appropriate page or pages.

Downstairs, Ethel Kennedy slowly regained her breath, lowered herself from the cabinet, and walked, unsteadily, out the back door. Sue Markham volunteered to take her to a nearby doctor who could examine and treat the wounds. A secretary summoned a veterinarian to capture the coati mundi, temporarily locked in a storeroom.

In the middle of the confusion, a horse van bearing Sargent Shriver's name drew up to the Kennedy home, and a young man began to unload tables and chairs. The night before, while the senator labored on his speech, his brother-in-law, Shriver, a loyal member of the Johnson Administration, gave a party using Kennedy's tables and chairs.

When Ethel Kennedy returned from the doctor, her scratched legs bandaged and stained by antiseptics, she was smiling. She even waved goodbye to the coati mundi as it disappeared in the vet's car. Then she looked from her bandages to her husband, who was about to leave to deliver his controversial speech.

"If these are all the scars the Kennedys end up with by five o'clock," said Ethel cheerfully, "it'll be all right."

At noon, Bobby Kennedy kissed his wife goodbye, slipped into a white Oldsmobile convertible in the driveway, and motioned his chauffeur, Jim Boyd, to the jump seat. Then Kennedy lowered the top of the convertible, and he drove. He drove fast, very fast. "If you want to get rid of your secretary," Angie Novello, shivering in the crisp air, yelled from the back seat, "just fire her. You don't have to do this."

Racing along the George Washington highway, Kennedy reached speeds of eighty miles an hour, almost certainly without realizing it, and when he crossed from Virginia into Washington, he took the bridge and the following curves at speeds well beyond the legal limit. He cruised through one red light near his office, his mind far from the road.

Yet when he pulled to the curb next to the New Senate Office Building, instead of rushing inside, Kennedy paused to climb aboard a bus filled with school chil-

Frank Mankiewicz, Kennedy's press secretary, stayed up all night, too.

"Theodore Sorensen, once special counsel to John F. Kennedy, read one draft, edited it, and returned it to Kennedy."

dren, white and Negro, from Prince George County, Virginia. He joked with the children and invited them to visit him. Then, buoyed by their enthusiasm, he hurried to his suite of offices on the ground floor of the New Senate Office Building.

Walinsky and Edelman, both of whose politics lean to the left of Kennedy's, sat at their desks, studying the text of the speech. A copy of Edmund Burke's *On Conciliation* lay on Walinsky's desk, open to a quote Walinsky had inserted into the speech: "Conciliation failing, force remains; but, force failing, no further hope of reconciliation is left."

Kennedy approached Edelman, who had come to work despite a strep throat. "Am I a big enough dove for you, Peter?" the senator asked.

Edelman looked up from the speech. "No," he said.

"Good," said Kennedy, grinning. "That makes me feel better."

Kennedy vanished into his private office and began examining the speech once more. Occasionally, Walinsky or Edelman or Mankiewicz burst in with a modest suggestion, a shift in wording, a new phrase. Walinsky and Edelman shared their small quarters with three typists; two prepared stencils for the mimeographed copies of the speech that would be distributed among the press and the Senate, while the other prepared a large-lettered speaking copy for the senator. In the reception room, overcrowded under normal circumstances, reporters and photographers jockeyed for position. The reporters had been promised copies of the text before noon—"We'll send up puffs of white smoke if it's dovish, gray if it's hawkish," Mankiewicz had said—but at 12:45 p.m. they still had not seen a word.

At 12:50 p.m., a bell rang signaling a minor roll-call vote on the floor of the Senate. Prodded by Walinsky, Kennedy emerged from his office, bounded outside, and walked briskly till he reached the base of the steps to the Capitol. Then someone shouted, "They're holding the vote for you," and the senator raced full-speed up the steps, Walinsky lagging in pursuit.

Kennedy registered his vote in favor of a motion to table an amendment to the Senate reform bill, then joined his brother Teddy for the walk back to their offices. Next to his taller, huskier brother, Bobby, five-feet-ten and 165 pounds, looked slight. As they started across the street, a teen-age girl rushed up with a camera. "Can I take a picture of the two of you?" she asked.

"No," said Bobby Kennedy. "The three of us. You get in the picture too." He handed the girl's camera to Walinsky, and, as the senators flanked the girl and flashed their brightest political smiles, Walinsky snapped the picture. The girl bubbled with delight.

Shortly after 1:30 p.m., reporters received their copies of the speech, marked "Hold for Delivery," and promptly started thumbing through the thirteen single-spaced pages. Some of the reporters found one of Kennedy's major points unclear, his call for a halt to the bombing and a simultaneous announcement that the United States would be ready to open negotiations within a week. Did the senator mean that if the communists did not come to the negotiating table within a week, the bombing should be resumed?

The senator did not. He meant that the bombing should be stopped indefinitely,

Peter Edelman, a legislative aide. " 'Am I a big enough dove for you, Peter?' "

until it became obvious that the communists had no desire to negotiate a peace. He carefully changed the text to emphasize the indefinite halt to the bombing.

As a matter of form, Kennedy dispatched a copy of his speech to the White House's Congressional liaison office, which passed it to Walt W. Rostow, the special assistant for national security affairs, who passed it, in turn, to the State Department. Lyndon Johnson himself did not take time to read the speech. The President already knew its substance—earlier in the week, he had sent representatives of the State Department, including Ambassador Averill Harriman, to try to dissuade Kennedy from delivering the speech—and, besides, his own schedule had suddenly grown remarkably hectic.

Late in the morning, after he knew for certain that Kennedy would speak in the afternoon, the President called an impromptu press conference in the White House, his second of the week, and spiced the conference with a major announcement: Premier Kosygin had agreed to discuss with the United States the possibility of limiting the nuclear-missile race.

Kennedy learned of the President's dramatic conference at 2 p.m. from two reporters friendly to his cause. "Do you think he really just heard from Kosygin today?" one of the reporters asked. "He couldn't have been saving that item, could he have?"

Kennedy smiled. He did not acknowledge aloud that the President might be seeking to upstage him. He did not have to. His smile told everything.

"Besides," said the other reporter, "Johnson's just scheduled two speeches for this afternoon, one at Howard University and one at the Office of Education. You suppose he just found out that it's the one hundredth anniversary of Howard?"

Kennedy smiled again.

"He's got buses to take the press to his speeches," the reporter continued. "He certainly is being considerate."

Kennedy's expression did not change.

At 2:30, the senator admitted half a dozen reporters to his private office to discuss the background to his speech. He sat, with his shirt sleeves rolled up, with his collar open and his tie loosened, in front of several water and finger paintings perpetrated by his children. Leather-bound volumes of his three books—*The Enemy Within*, based on his work investigating labor racketeering in the 1950s; *Just Friends and Brave Enemies*, based on his around-the-world goodwill trip in 1962; and *The Pursuit of Justice*, based on his term as Attorney General—and several of his brother's works rested on his desk. On one wall hung an oil painting entitled *Before His Last Mission*, a portrait of Joseph P. Kennedy Jr., Bobby's oldest brother, shortly before his plane blew up over the English Channel. On another wall hung the framed doodlings scribbled by John F. Kennedy during his final cabinet meeting, October 29, 1963—a gift "To Bob from Jacqueline."

"The President," said one reporter, after Kennedy briefly summarized the work that went into his speech, "makes the charge that speeches like this do a disservice to our boys overseas."

Kennedy considered his reply. "You have to balance that," he said, "against

Adam Walinsky, the chief staff speechwriter, worked up one draft of the speech more radical than Goodwin's.

33

Joseph Dolan, Kennedy's administrative assistant. " 'Stand up and talk. Don't apologize.' "

what you think does the greatest amount of good. I don't think we're going to end the war by military action."

"Do you think this'll make the President's job more difficult?"

Kennedy ducked the question. "I didn't speak for a year," he said. "I've tried every other way to show my feeling of responsibility."

"Do you have a sense of crossing the Rubicon?"

The senator grinned. "I've thought about it," he said. "I haven't had wide support for the political advisability of making this speech."

His hair fell toward his eyes, and as he spoke, he chewed gum.

"Do you think all that activity down at the White House is because of you?"

Kennedy pleaded innocent. "Why ask me?" he said.

"They're shelling the Capitol," one reporter suggested.

A green beret, the symbol of the Special Forces troops, sat on a ledge behind Kennedy's desk. It had been worn by an honor guard at John Kennedy's funeral.

"Would you say," Bobby was asked, "that the country today is more hawkish than dovish?"

"Yes," he said.

As the reporters stood to leave, one of them smiled and said, "Congratulations about Hoffa."

The following Tuesday, James R. Hoffa, the president of the International Brotherhood of Teamsters, and Kennedy's most bitter and persistent foe for a decade, was going to jail.

Kennedy, unable to resist the opening, turned impish. "Uh—as you know," he said, almost parodying his own accent, "I—uh—have never had a personal vendetta with Jimmy Hoffa. And—uh—anyway, I am—uh—not ruthless."

The reporters were replaced in Kennedy's office by the school children from Prince George County, Virginia, who had taken up his invitation. On the brink of his speech, Kennedy took time to greet and entertain the children. He also found time to change to a fresh white shirt—plucked out of the supply always on hand—and to comb his rumpled hair. Then, at 3:20, dressed in a two-button dark blue suit, Kennedy left his office, joined his brother on the sidewalk, and walked off to deliver his speech.

As Kennedy rose to speak at 3:40 p.m., some twenty-five senators sat in the chamber, the largest gathering to hear a speech in several weeks, but still only a quarter of the membership and fewer than half as many senators as listened to Kennedy's first major Senate speech, in June, 1965, on nuclear proliferation. At least three of the Democratic senators in attendance—Majority Leader Mike Mansfield of Montana, J. William Fulbright of Arkansas, and George McGovern of South Dakota—knew what to expect; Kennedy had called and briefed each of them. At least two freshman Republican senators—Charles H. Percy of Illinois and Edward W. Brooke of Massachusetts—listened with more than polite interest; each had already indicated his displeasure with the conduct of the war in Vietnam. (Brooke later shifted toward the Administration, Percy further away.) Several senators sat in the chamber simply because it was convenient; they had just finished a roll-call vote and they lingered only long enough to hear the start of the speech.

Bobby Kennedy's first few words—"Ten thousand miles from this chamber we are engaged in . . ."—came out flatly, quietly, lost in the Senate din. But, soon, the chamber settled down, and the loudest sound, except for the senator's measured tones, was the turning of pages by people following the prepared text. The gallery was well populated, particularly in the press section, but not full. Ethel Kennedy, her legs bandaged but her natural good spirits returned, sat with a few friends in the family section of the gallery. Perhaps half the senator's full-time Washington office staff of thirty-two listened, some in the family gallery, most in the staff gallery. Mankiewicz and Walinsky roamed the floor of the Senate, Edelman sat in the family gallery, and Kennedy's third legislative assistant, the last one to join the office, Wendell Pigman, sat in the staff gallery.

Kennedy trod softly at the beginning, sprinkling into his text the necessary patriotic shorthand, paying the required homage to the goodwill of the President and the goodwill of the American people. He acknowledged, predictably, the complexity of the war and the painful responsibilities borne by the President, and he warned that the enemy should not mistake debate for division. "Three Presidents have taken action in Vietnam," he said. "As one who was involved in many of those decisions, I can testify that if fault is to be found . . . there is enough to go around for all—including myself."

In gently criticizing himself, the senator was not only being tactful; he was being accurate. "We will win in Vietnam and we shall remain here until we do," he had said in Saigon in 1962, and his tone at the time had clearly implied a military victory.

Now, for several minutes, his speech followed a conventional path. He insisted that every senator desired peace, that the President had worked mightily to achieve a negotiated peace, that the fault for the absence of peace lay largely with the communists. Then, smoothly and unmistakably, Kennedy began to move toward his separate position, toward criticism of the Johnson Administration's strategy for peace.

"If this war was not our doing, and it is not our fault," he said, "still it is partly our responsibility. . . . Let us reflect for a moment not on the wisdom and necessity of our cause nor on the valor of the South Vietnamese, but on the horror. . . . For although the world's imperfections may call forth the acts of war, righteousness cannot obscure the agony and pain those acts bring to a single child. The Vietnamese war is an event of historic moment, summoning the grandeur and concern of many nations. But it is also the vacant moment of amazing fear as a mother and child watch death fall by fire from the improbable machine sent by a country they barely comprehend. . . . It is the young men, Vietnamese and American, who in an instant sense the night of death destroying yesterday's promise. . . . It is a land deafened by the unending crescendo of violence, hatred, and savage fury. . . .

"All we say and all we do must be informed by our awareness that this horror is partly our responsibility. . . . It is we who live in abundance and send our young men out to die. It is our chemicals that scorch the children and our bombs that level the villages. . . ."

Ed Guthman, formerly Kennedy's press secretary at the Justice Department and currently National Editor of the Los Angeles Times, *was consulted about the speech, as he is about practically every other major (and minor) matter.*

35

R. F. K.

Angela Novello, Kennedy's personal secretary since 1957, typed through the night.

Kennedy outlined the costliness of the war, its destructive impact upon South Vietnam, its damaging effect upon American-Soviet relations, its burgeoning demand for funds that might otherwise be used to fight poverty and aid education in the United States.

Briefly, Senator Fulbright interrupted to add his assessment of the damaging side effects of the war, whereupon Senator Gale McGee of Wyoming interrupted to disagree with Fulbright, and Senator Joseph Clark of Pennsylvania interrupted to disagree with McGee. Then Senator Frank Lausche of Ohio said he found ambiguities in Kennedy's text and began asking questions about points Kennedy had not yet covered.

"Would the senator permit me to continue . . .?" Kennedy asked.

". . . I, for one, would like to see him continue," said Majority Leader Mansfield.

"I would not have interrupted . . .," said Lausche, "had not the senator from Arkansas started the discussion."

"I withdraw the interruption," said Fulbright, laughing.

Kennedy resumed his speech, and now, slipping in a Biblical allusion and another mild tribute to Lyndon Johnson, he moved to his main points.

"The steps I am suggesting are intimately related," he said. "They stand together, each dependent on the other. It will do little good to go to the conference table if discussions are simply used to mask continued escalation of the war. Nor will negotiations be fruitful unless they lead to a reasonable and honorable settlement with some hope of lasting peace.

"Therefore, I propose we test the sincerity of the statements by Premier Kosygin and others asserting that if the bombardment of the North is halted, negotiations would begin—by halting the bombardment and saying we are ready to negotiate within the week, making it clear that discussions cannot continue for a prolonged period without an agreement that neither side will substantially increase the size of the war in South Vietnam—by infiltration or reinforcement. An international group should be asked to inspect the borders and ports of the country to report any further escalation. And under the directions of the United Nations, and with an international presence gradually replacing American forces, we should move toward a final settlement which allows all the major political elements in South Vietnam to participate in the choice of leadership and shape their future direction as a people."

Robert Kennedy's three-point plan—ending the bombing in the North, ending the escalation in the South, and starting toward full and free elections in the South —seemed neither terribly dramatic nor especially revolutionary. Similar proposals had already been advanced by, among others, Senators Clark of Pennsylvania and Wayne Morse of Oregon. Yet their arguments, even if equally eloquent and reasoned, were scarcely noted, simply because neither of them, so predictably liberal, could command the same national attention, and curiosity, as the forty-one-year-old junior senator from New York. Neither was named Kennedy.

Kennedy went on to explain his proposals more thoroughly, amplifying the advantages and seeking to anticipate the rebuttals. He flavored his lengthy talk—his large-lettered speaking copy ran 104 pages—with the almost ritualistic references to his late brother's thoughts and deeds, with quotations from Franklin Roosevelt and Bernard Shaw, with comments from Robert McNamara and Harold Wilson.

When Kennedy finished, the Majority Leader opened discussion of the speech. "I compliment and commend the senator," Mansfield began, "on a most thoughtful and soul-searching speech . . . not . . . easy . . . to make, but . . . necessary. . . . There will be those who will read into it a divergence, a difference, between the senator from New York and the Administration."

Mansfield proceeded to close the gap, praising Kennedy's "calm and dispassionate tone . . . free of rancor," minimizing the conflict between the senator and the President. "This is a good and a sound subject to discuss at any time . . .," Mansfield concluded, "and to do so in the constructive manner which the senator from New York has undertaken to do this afternoon is most worthy of the Senate in its best moments."

After Senator Fulbright, not surprisingly, lauded the speech, Senator Lausche, in disagreement, argued that the communists demanded, as a precondition to bargaining, a permanent halt to the bombing of the North, and that the United States could not afford to promise a permanent halt. When Lausche quoted a message from Ho Chi Minh to Pope Paul—"The United States must unconditionally and definitively stop the bombing"—and then said, "Ho Chi Minh says that we must stop it permanently and unconditionally," Kennedy pounced upon Lausche with the cross-examining instinct he had sharpened during his years as counsel to Senator Joseph McCarthy's and Senator John McClellan's investigating committees.

"Did the senator from Ohio," Kennedy asked, "describe the message to the Pope, a moment ago, as saying 'permanently'?"

"Yes," said Lausche.

"What words did he use?"

"He said," Lausche repeated, "'The United States must unconditionally and definitively stop the bombing.'"

"Did he use the word 'permanently'?" Kennedy pressed.

"No, he did not," Lausche conceded. "But . . . 'definitively' means an end . . . and that is what he meant by this statement."

"It is of interest, though," Kennedy countered, with obvious satisfaction, "that he in fact did not use the word 'permanently.'"

A few minutes later, Senator Henry Jackson of Washington took the floor and began to criticize the first step in Kennedy's plan, his call for a halt in the bombing. Jackson insisted that several times before, the United States had stopped its raids on the North and each time the communists had shown no willingness to come to the negotiating table. Kennedy argued that the previous pauses had come in a less hopeful atmosphere, that the New Year's pauses had been accompanied by infiltration on one side and reinforcement on the other, that now, judging from Premier Kosygin's statement, the mood was promising.

Jackson and Kennedy debated in circles, each holding his ground, neither conceding a point. It seemed ironic that the two should be so diametrically opposed; they knew each other well. In 1954, thirteen years earlier, a dispute over Senator Jackson almost triggered a fist fight between Kennedy and Roy Cohn, Senator Joseph McCarthy's chief counsel; Kennedy defended Jackson. And in 1960, when John F. Kennedy won the Presidential nomination, Bobby Kennedy favored Henry Jackson over Lyndon Johnson for the Vice-Presidential nomination.

But now, on the Senate floor, Henry Jackson, who might have been President had Bobby Kennedy had his way, was strongly supporting Lyndon Johnson. Suddenly, to Kennedy's evident surprise, Jackson stopped arguing and came to the point of his interruption. He wished to place in the *Congressional Record* a letter from Lyndon Johnson. "I had asked the President at a dinner on February 18 last," Jackson said, "to indicate the Administration's position on the bombing."

Almost as if by cue, Senator George Smathers of Florida popped to his feet. "Would the senator from Washington mind telling us what is in that letter?" said Smathers.

"Will the senator from New York," Jackson said, "yield further to me for the purpose of reading this letter?"

"I am happy to yield to the senator from Washington for that purpose," said Kennedy, his happiness not fully convincing.

By coincidence, the letter was dated the previous day, March 1, 1967, and al-

" 'Make sure that they announce it's the Kennedy from New York.' "

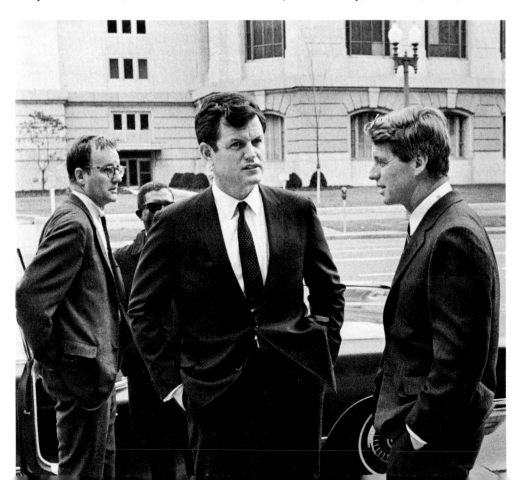

ready, while Kennedy had been delivering his speech, Jackson had distributed mimeographed copies of Lyndon Johnson's letter to the press. The President was maneuvering magnificently.

Kennedy exchanges views with reporters after his speech in the Senate.

Basically, the letter justified the bombing and the entire Administration position in Vietnam. As Jackson read, Kennedy paced, sometimes folding his arms across his chest, sometimes rubbing his chin, listening to the President's counterattack.

By this time, close to 6 p.m., barely a dozen senators remained in the chamber, and as a few more drifted out, Teddy Kennedy hailed a page and asked him to deliver a scribbled note to his brother. "I'm not leaving," the note explained, "because I'm afraid to go outside."

After Jackson's performance, Senator McGee of Wyoming resumed an earlier debate with Kennedy, a debate focusing upon whether or not the communists had actually given any signal that they might be willing to negotiate. Kennedy interpreted Kosygin's statement as sufficient signal, but McGee was not satisfied; both agreed that a neon sign was unnecessary.

In the past, McGee, like Jackson, had often fought on Kennedy's side. "There is a new frontier in the Senate," he had said, after Kennedy's first year as a senator. "There is the attrition of time and the momentum of change around the country— and it may permit the flowering of a Kennedy leadership."

Now, Kennedy stood with his arms folded across his chest and stared steadily at McGee. Behind Kennedy, Adam Walinsky loyally stood with his arms folded across his chest and stared steadily at McGee.

At 6:30 p.m. the debate ended. It had been spirited, but not greatly enlightening or greatly constructive. Only one Republican, John Sherman Cooper of Kentucky, had spoken, and he had endorsed the speech. Senators McGovern, Clark, Claiborne Pell of Rhode Island, Albert Gore of Tennessee, and Joseph Tydings of Maryland added their support; Senator Robert Byrd of West Virginia politely dissented. But no one struck to the heart of the matter, the twin real dangers of Bobby Kennedy's speech:

(1) Because of his running ideological and political dispute with the President—a dispute so deep that the President could not easily accept Kennedy's proposals even if he agreed with them—Kennedy risked inspiring escalation by condemning escalation.

(2) Because the President seemed increasingly committed to a military victory, or at least to a display of military superiority so overwhelming that it would force the communists to negotiate, and because the communists might wishfully cling to Kennedy's speech as evidence that American military pressure would eventually be relaxed, Kennedy risked prolonging the war by calling for its end.

Kennedy recognized both risks, but he felt that his moral and tactical obligations to speak outweighed them. He recognized too that his name exaggerated the coverage given his words and, simultaneously perhaps, as a result of the political machinations, reduced the thought given his words.

He paused briefly to repeat sections of his speech for the television cameras, then left the Capitol, a little less jaunty than when he had arrived, a little tired. The number of senators in attendance and the length of the debate, he said, had pleasantly surprised him. He particularly appreciated Mansfield's comments. "A real stand-up guy," Kennedy said.

One of his aides slyly suggested that Kennedy send Senator Jackson a gift: "Why not send him the coati mundi?"

When Kennedy entered his office, Angie Novello greeted him with a congratulatory kiss on his cheek. He made a few phone calls, quickly changed his shirt once more, and hurried to the airport; as little as he liked the idea, he had to catch the shuttle to New York to attend a political testimonial dinner. As he passed a newsstand at the airport, he noticed a late edition of *The Washington Star* with front-page stories about his speech and Lyndon Johnson's press conference. He indicated that he would like to see the paper. He also indicated that he did not have a dime. A reporter bought the paper for him.

When the stewardess came to collect fares during the flight to New York, everyone paid, as expected on the shuttle, by cash, check, or credit card—everyone except Kennedy. "Would you send me a bill?" he said.

"Certainly," said the stewardess, and she began filling out a form. She did not ask his name. "Your address, please?"

"New Senate Office Building," said Kennedy.

"Would you like a copy of the bill?" the stewardess offered.

Everyone keeps copies of his bills. "No thanks," said Bobby.

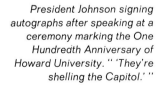

President Johnson signing autographs after speaking at a ceremony marking the One Hundredth Anniversary of Howard University. " 'They're shelling the Capitol.' "

As he read his mail and a few newspapers, Kennedy rested his feet casually in the aisle. Once a stewardess stumbled over him. "Excuse me," she said when she regained her balance.

The senator, without looking up, said nothing.

His Manhattan limousine met him at the airport, and Kennedy offered a ride to two reporters and a young folksinger he had just met. The folksinger, Phil Ochs, had flown to Washington specifically to hear Kennedy's speech.

"Is it true," the senator asked, "that Bob Dylan changed his name to help his career?"

"Yes," said Ochs.

Kennedy smiled. "You think it would help me," he said, "if I changed mine?"

Already, the President's well-orchestrated counterinsurgency campaign was at work against Kennedy. Within a few hours after the speech, Secretary of State Dean Rusk issued a statement rejecting the validity of Kennedy's proposals. "There is . . . no reason," Rusk said, "to believe at this time that Hanoi is interested in proposals for mutual de-escalation such as those put forward by Senator Kennedy."

The chairman of the House Armed Services Committee, L. Mendel Rivers of South Carolina, followed with his own attack. "You can bet your bottom dollar," Rivers snapped, that the United States would not benefit from a halt in the bombing. The Minority Leader of the Senate, Everett Dirksen of Illinois, voiced his opposition, and Representative Emanuel Celler of Brooklyn, usually a Kennedy ally, said he found the senator's proposals "foolhardy." *The New York Times*, after internal debate, played Kennedy's speech more prominently than Johnson's press conference, and supported Kennedy's sentiments, but, generally, the President won the war of words. Reaction across the country ran heavily against Kennedy's ideas and his timing, and his popularity noticeably suffered.

Eventually, Lyndon Johnson joined the assault himself. In a speech before the Tennessee legislature, he vigorously defended his policy in Vietnam and, almost sarcastically, stressed the futility of halting the bombing as a step toward peace. Kennedy, with several of his aides, watched the President's speech on television, and when Johnson slipped and talked about shifting the conflict from the "battle-field to the battle box," instead of "ballot box," a few members of the Kennedy staff laughed. When the President said, "Now, as to bombing civilians, I would simply say that we're making an effort . . . unprecedented in the history of warfare to be sure that we do not," a few of the Kennedy people looked incredulous. Kennedy studied the TV screen carefully. He did not say a word aloud against Lyndon Johnson, yet his feelings came through vividly. Affection was not among them.

"I had a nice meeting with the President this week," Kennedy told a banquet audience a week after his Vietnam speech. "We talked about a ceasefire, escalation, and prospects of negotiations for peace."

Bobby Kennedy hesitated for a second, then added: "And he said when I come back next time we might talk about Vietnam."

CHAPTER THREE

THE PACKAGE AND THE PRODUCT

". . . As our population increases, as the problems of our society become more complex, and as the cost of political campaigns continues to mount—it becomes more and more clear that the package is often more important than the product, that the perceived image of a candidate is often more important than what he says. . . ."

—Robert F. Kennedy
February 22, 1967

Robert F. Kennedy comes in a handsome package. Youthful, vigorous, good-looking, elegantly wrapped in pertinent statistics and proper causes, brightly decorated by experience in almost every phase of governmental activity, Bobby Kennedy looks like the perfect present for the country that has everything. The difficulties begin when one opens the package.

Inside the outer box, there is another box, and inside that, another, and another, like an unending practical joke, until, finally, one reaches the core, the product. There is a core—a basic Bobby Kennedy who believes in good and evil, who loves and hates, who is capable of the extreme emotions, the genuine emotions. Immediately, this puts Bobby Kennedy ahead of so many politicians who are only boxes inside boxes—fewer and far less fascinating boxes than surround Bobby Kennedy—with nothing at the core.

Yet the boxes that surround Kennedy are more than decoration. They are significant. Each reveals a facet of his personality, a facet of his past, and each has a bearing on all he says and all he does. With Bobby Kennedy, to a very real extent, to twist the message of Marshall McLuhan, the product is the package.

Ultimately, the analogy grows complicated, which is only fitting, because Bobby Kennedy is a complicated man. Someone once said that he is not a complicated man, that, rather, he is several simple men, but even this is oversimplifica-

The Package. "Ruthless or compassionate? Brash or shy? Detached or involved? Devious or honest? Opportunist or idealist? Vacuous or intelligent?" This photograph, greatly enlarged, is widely sold to adolescents and other followers along with posters of Humphrey Bogart, Paul Newman, and The Monkees.

45

tion. It is almost impossible to generalize about Bobby Kennedy, and at the same time it is almost impossible to feel neutral about him. He inspires only the most forceful reactions. His friends, in their analyses, elevate him to the brink of sainthood; his enemies, in turn, condemn him to the inner circles of hell. Even the people who feel ambivalently about him express their ambivalence in the strongest possible terms, offering him, simultaneously, the ultimate in acceptance and the ultimate in rejection. "I'd sleep with him," says one woman reporter who has observed him often, "but I wouldn't vote for him."

Even the simplest, most elementary facts about Bobby Kennedy allow vastly differing interpretations. Consider, for example, his eyes. He has two of them, and both are very blue and very light, and neither is exceptional. Yet, while they suggest nothing but ice to anyone who has crossed him, they are beautiful beyond description to a young girl who works for him. Or consider his physique, which is lean, almost bony, not extraordinary. Still he looks ruggedly wiry to one person, vulnerably frail to another. Once one moves past the sheer physical traits into subjective areas, the contradictions, of course, become more pronounced. Just as his eyes can freeze or melt, he can be judged ruthless or compassionate, brash or shy, detached or involved, devious or honest, opportunist or idealist, vacuous or intelligent. Bobby Kennedy is a festival of antonyms.

One newspaperman who was close to John F. Kennedy, who has known Bobby Kennedy well for more than a decade and has felt both Bobby's warmth and Bobby's heat, neatly verbalizes the conflict. "Just when you get Bobby typed," he says, "as the white hope, bright and compassionate and vibrant and with it, he'll do something so bad it'll jar you completely, destroy your faith in him. And just as you're ready to accept the excessive condemnations, to accept him as ruthless and diabolical, he'll do something so classy it stuns you.

"In many ways, he is more interesting than John Kennedy, more paradoxical. It is harder to get at the true Robert Kennedy than the true John Kennedy."

The inescapable truth about Robert Kennedy is that the paradoxes are real, the conflicts do exist. There is a good Bobby and a bad Bobby, a fairly good Bobby and a fairly bad Bobby, all tangled together, and the responsibility is to look for the balance. So many people do not. They purchase only the package of Kennedy they want.

The most impassioned and vociferous of the anti-Bobby voices are those, ironically, of people who, like himself, have taken up a position to the left of the national consensus. They don't like his company, and they give him no credit for being there. Essentially, their antagonism springs from an instinct that is simple and understandable, if open to debate: They do not trust him. Lacking trust, they doubt his motives, and by finding him opportunistic, devious, insincere, they pronounce him a false liberal.

"It is apparent," wrote playwright-essayist Gore Vidal, a voice of the middle-aged moderate left, who gets furious whenever he hears Bobby Kennedy's name, "that Bobby's view of men and actions is a good deal closer to that of Barry Goldwater than it is to that of his brother."

The Product. "There is a core — a basic Bobby Kennedy who believes in good and evil, who loves and hates, who is capable of the extreme emotions, the genuine emotions. Immediately, this puts Bobby Kennedy ahead of so many politicians."

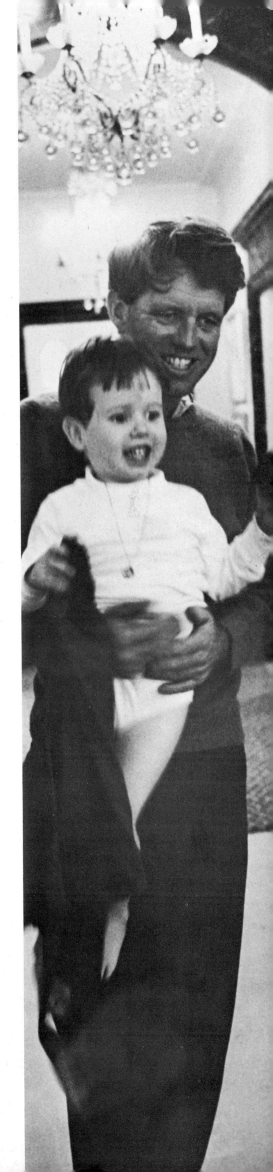

R. F. K.

"The Kennedy rhetoric is dangerous," wrote journalist Robert Scheer, a voice of the young New Left, "precisely because it provides the illusion of dissent without its substance. Hubert Humphrey is a bad joke to most young people, but Bobby is believable, and for that reason, much more serious. He could easily co-opt prevailing dissent without delivering to it. In fact, much of his magic lies in his ability to convince potential critics that they are part of an entourage of trusted aides to a beneficent but insurgent crown prince. . . .

"Commitment to a moral imperative, political idealism, or even the integrity of a western's high noon are things he can admire from afar, but they are not now a part of his own world. He respects Yevtushenko whom he has met, but he would rather be Kosygin, whom he very likely detests. Stokely Carmichael is admired for his courage, but Roy Wilkins is the figure to deal with. The verve of Mario Savio is appealing to him, but it is to Clark Kerr that he looks for human progress."

The anti-Bobby liberals lift most of their specific criticisms out of his past, then blend them with their own suspicions about the present. Asked to present an indictment of Kennedy, they reach back to the influence of his unmistakably conservative father, to his service for and his friendship with Senator Joseph McCarthy, to his ruthless, if righteous, crusade against Jimmy Hoffa and the Teamsters Union. Because solid contemporary evidence is more elusive, they turn subjective, reasoning that Bobby Kennedy, like all men, must be the product of his past, that he leans left now only for expediency, that his words ring hollow, that his actions do not even measure up to his words. Sometimes, armed with evidence and emotion, they unleash vicious attacks on Kennedy—Vidal's cattiness is classic: "He's a dangerous, ruthless man. He's a Torquemada-like personality. . . . It would take a public-relations genius to make him appear lovable. He is not. His obvious characteristics are energy, vindictiveness, and a simple-mindedness about human motives which may yet bring him down"—but their character assassinations are not nearly so significant, ultimately, as their doubts. Their doubts about Bobby Kennedy's sincerity are often genuine, and reasonable men who do not deal in vituperation, who would not stoop to flinging labels, share their doubts.

But there is an army at work seeking to dispel the doubts, people who welcome Kennedy to their position left of center, who enjoy his company. And their enthusiasm springs, like the antagonism, from a basic instinct: They trust Bobby Kennedy. They accept him as a true convert to their cause, and they judge him to be, like so many converts, a more fervent believer than the originals.

THESE ARE THE BOBBY TWINS. ONE IS A GOOD BOBBY. ONE IS A BAD BOBBY. 1.

THE GOOD BOBBY IS A COURAGEOUS REFORMER. THE BAD BOBBY MAKES DEALS. 2.

THE GOOD BOBBY SENT FEDERAL TROOPS DOWN SOUTH TO ENFORCE CIVIL RIGHTS. THE BAD BOBBY APPOINTED RACIST JUDGES DOWN SOUTH TO ENFORCE CIVIL RIGHTS. 3.

"Kennedy has worked for his liberalism," sociologist Daniel Patrick Moynihan, another voice of the middle-aged moderate left, has suggested. "It's not something he learned at the Bronx High School of Science. The things he learned first were conservative things. The things he learned second were liberal things. He is an idealist without illusions. He is committed to a certain kind of tough-mindedness. You might want to call this the higher liberalism."

"Kennedy is the first liberal politician," wrote journalist Jack Newfield, another voice of the young New Left, "to transcend the cold war and the clichés of the 1950s. He is more concerned with peace treaties than with collective security; more involved with the non-working poor than with the labor-union bureaucracy; more attuned to the Negro's need for participation and pride in his blackness than to the old slogans of integration. He is totally contemporary."

Awash in the Hatch River.

THE GOOD BOBBY IS A FERVENT CIVIL LIBERTARIAN.

THE BAD BOBBY IS A FERVENT WIRE TAPPER.

4.

THE GOOD BOBBY IS ILL AT EASE WITH LIBERALS.

THE BAD BOBBY IS ILL AT EASE WITH GROWNUPS.

5.

IF YOU WANT ONE BOBBY TO BE YOUR PRESIDENT YOU WILL HAVE TO TAKE BOTH...

FOR BOBBIES ARE WIDELY NOTED FOR THEIR FAMILY UNITY.

6.

The pro-Bobby liberals recognize his past, acknowledge the McCarthy-Hoffa syndrome, but discount it as part of his maturing process. They cull the evidence for their support of him from his more recent statements and actions, his resistance to an air strike against Cuba, his stand against the conduct of the war in Vietnam, his battles to enroll James Meredith at the University of Mississippi and to enroll thousands of Negro voters in the South, his expanding concern for the civil liberties of the individual, his expressed conviction that the radicals of the right pose a greater threat to the United States today than the radicals of the left. Like their anti-Bobby counterparts, they, too, mix evidence and emotion to a boiling point—Arthur Schlesinger Jr. wrote: "No doubt Robert's first political heroes were Herbert Hoover and Douglas MacArthur; no doubt he once considered Yalta a national betrayal; no doubt he regarded (and continued to regard) professional liberals with suspicion. But in my experience he did not hold grudges, cherish a black-and-white view of life, scorn issues of personal freedom or believe that anyone who was not with him was against him. . . . Indeed . . . what seemed most characteristic were his gentleness, consideration, idealism, and, if the word had not been hopelessly degraded by political oratory, compassion"—but the important point is that they accept him.

Beyond acceptance, some liberals see Bobby Kennedy as a man who can bring liberalism a winning spirit, a success it never before possessed. "If you get to know most American liberals," Pat Moynihan said, "you find there's a tremendous streak of softness that likes to lose. Their judgments of reality are confirmed by loss. Kennedy does not have this quality and does not admire it. For example, he went to the headquarters of William Fitts Ryan on primary night [during the 1965 New York mayoral race], saw the happy throngs, and said, 'My God, you'd think they'd won.' That seemed to him aberrant behavior."

Outside the liberal community Bobby Kennedy generates equal heat but less debate. Most people who lean toward the conservative are united against him, and they do not have to persuade each other. They go mostly by gut reaction—the label of "left-wing Democrat" is sufficient—because they are unable to strike at certain vulnerable points, like his ties with McCarthy. For this reason, an attack upon Bobby Kennedy from the right is liable to look ludicrous. In his destructive biography, *RFK: The Man Who Would Be President*, Ralph de Toledano thoroughly skewers Kennedy ("I couldn't find a kind word in it," said the senator, after a quick perusal), but his arguments grow confused and dull. The book does cover the conservative complaints with Kennedy—his statements on Vietnam and Red China and nuclear proliferation give body to predictable conservative cries of "soft on communism" and "appeaser"—but the complaints lose impact because de Toledano, unwilling to concede Kennedy anything, points out that some liberals do not believe Kennedy. He tries to have at Kennedy both ways, and he can't; the law-enforcement officer in Kennedy, and the investigator in him, appeal to conservatives, but de Toledano, in his fury, attacks even these traits and adopts the liberal line. Ultimately, he depends heavily upon the ammunition of the left, and so heavily upon finding personality faults—arrogance, ruthlessness, and

" 'The Kennedy rhetoric is dangerous precisely because it provides the illusion of dissent without its substance.' "

53

vindictiveness—that he must resort, at one point, to condemning Kennedy because the senator allows Brumus, the giant Newfoundland, to climb all over guests at Hickory Hill.

Kennedy does have some conservative supporters—ideological conservatives who detest Gore Vidal but share his belief that Bobby Kennedy is basically conservative; reflex conservatives who, ignoring ideology, want to exorcise the national guilt about the assassination of John F. Kennedy; Roman Catholics who accept Kennedy strictly on the basis of religion. They are a distinct minority.

54

Within the Washington Establishment, considerable anti-Bobby sentiment flourishes, fed not by any ideology, but by a resentment of anyone who flagrantly violates the rules of the game. Kennedy is a member of the Democratic Party who flouts the Democratic leadership. He is a junior senator who refuses to behave like a junior senator. He is obviously impatient, obviously eager to rock the political boat, and to men who have built careers upon tact and discretion, he appears rash and impolite. They are as angry at Bobby Kennedy because his Vietnam speech undermined the government position—totally aside from the

55

merits of the position—as they are because he may have delivered it for his own political reasons.

Of course, pro-Bobby people exist within the Establishment, Kennedyites in Johnsonian clothing, even some who look kindly upon both the President and the senator, who can sympathize with each's problems and each's ambitions. One of the central points about Bobby Kennedy is that neither political stance nor political position absolutely predetermines anyone's feelings toward him, a point emphasizing, once again, that one's view of Kennedy depends so much upon one's angle of vision—accidental or deliberate. The Kennedy-watcher is partly like a spectator at a boxing match who, no matter where he sits, may miss seeing one fighter throw a low punch or the other land a clean blow; and he is partly like a man lost in love, who chooses to see only the beauty, not the blemishes, or a man lost in hate, who chooses to see only the reverse. Distance does not sharpen the view. There are European socialists who see Kennedy—the million-aire's son who still has difficulty absorbing abstract notions—as an intellectual socialist; there are other European socialists who see Kennedy, just as clearly, as an unprincipled capitalist-colonialist.

It seems incredible that one man could inspire such opposite assessments, but examine the levels of Bobby Kennedy, the boxes that surround him, and the conflicts become understandable. Start with a level immediately evident. Start with his charisma. Beyond a doubt, he has charisma, an almost magical drawing power that prompts construction workers, balanced on the girders of a skeletal building, to wave at him as he walks by, that pulls teenagers away from their transistors and gathers them about him, that turns college students into squealing maniacs. No one who has ever traveled with him can doubt his appeal. People want to see him, touch him, smile at him, shake his hand, even rumple his hair, and his supporters say he is a symbol of the dynamic new politics, and his detrac-tors say he is trading on the reputation of his dead brother.

Certainly, the legacy-legend of J.F.K. lends itself to Bobby Kennedy's charisma. And, certainly, he encourages the connection inescapably, with his looks and voice and gestures, and, pointedly, with his repeated allusions to the martyred President. (Always, he refers to "President Kennedy" or "my brother"—never to "Jack." If anyone talks of the late President as "Jack" in Bobby Kennedy's presence, he winces, and the eyes do turn cold.) Critics suspect a ploy; friends consider the references a logical obsession. The first few times one hears Bobby Kennedy speak in public, and catches the insistent references to "President Kennedy," the suspicions seem reasonable. The references are often not essen-tial; they are sometimes irrelevent. But then, in private conversations, the same theme keeps coming through, the same quiet allusions, and then obviously it is not a ploy, and the best explanation seems to be that Bobby Kennedy quotes his brother the way a good preacher quotes the Bible. It is his favorite, most dependable text.

Each aspect of Bobby Kennedy's personality allows a similiar range of inter-pretations. He is, for instance, a notably disconcerting conversationalist; in the

" 'Kennedy is the first liberal politician to transcend the cold war and the clichés of the 1950s.' "

art of small talk, he is, at best, a few steps in front of the late Harpo Marx. "When you're with Bob," says William vanden Heuvel, a former Justice Department lawyer who serves as one of Kennedy's ties to New York politics, "the burden of conversation is always on you." The first temptation is to brand him distant or rude; the eventual realization that he is, actually, shy comes as a shock. No one should have his power and prestige, and still be shy. But Bobby Kennedy is. Additionally, suggests Peter Edelman, "The senator uses a shorthand in conversation. He doesn't waste words. It can be frustrating; you have to catch on fast."

Even the way his friends and associates refer to Kennedy is revealing. Edelman calls him "the senator"; vanden Heuvel, "Bob"; Schlesinger, "Robert." Each says "Kennedy" at times, and none says "Bobby." The diminutive, once used by everyone, is now reserved for his family. One explanation is that, when Jimmy Hoffa started calling him "Bobby" with heavy sarcasm, the name became distasteful to him. Another explanation is that "Bobby" sounds undignified for a

R. F. K.

United States senator in his forties. Neither explanation stands up. He looks like Bobby Kennedy, he sounds like Bobby Kennedy, he acts like Bobby Kennedy, and while his associates are saying "Bob" and "Robert" and "the senator," the guess is that they are thinking "Bobby."

The most legitimate reason for avoiding the diminutive is that "Bobby" connotes warmth, and Bobby Kennedy does not. To anyone who knows him less than intimately, Bobby Kennedy is not one of the warm people. He is not the sort of

person who immediately puts others at ease and encourages closeness. Yet he shows flashes of compassion that many of the warmest people cannot match.

Once, in a Kansas City suburb, only a few months after his brother's assassination, he dedicated a home for the aged, and Ben Bradlee, an objective Kennedy-watcher who is now the managing editor of *The Washington Post*, accompanied him. "The old and the crippled were all lined up downstairs," Bradlee recalls, "and after he spoke with them, he went upstairs where the dying were. There was

R.F.K.

A barrio in Brazil.

this woman rattling. It was the death rattle. I had never heard it before. Bob stood for twenty minutes holding her hand and whispering to her. She had no idea who he was. Bob was absolutely lost in this. No phoniness. No one around. No photographers. It brought tears to my eyes."

More recently, early in 1967, Kennedy visited a school for mentally retarded children in upstate New York. A little blonde girl, with that dreadful lost look in her eyes, turned away from him as he entered her room, and an attendant apologized, "She's shy." Kennedy smiled. "So am I," he said. A little boy awkwardly danced the twist for Kennedy, and the senator held his hand, and patted it, and said, "That's better than I can do." The little boy did not want to take his hand away from Kennedy's, and for perhaps a full minute, Kennedy stood still and rubbed the small hand. As he was leaving, one of the children shuffled up to him and handed him a fountain pen, and the senator thanked him warmly, and then, when he was away from the institution, he said, "Did you see that teacher hand the boy the pen to give to me? Wasn't that terrible?" The sham bothered him, and so did even the hint that someone might think the gift of a fountain pen would influence his feeling for the children and for the institution.

(opposite page, top left) Campaigning in New York. (top right) With children in Peru. (lower right) in the Mississippi Delta. " 'He is more concerned with peace treaties than with collective security; more involved with the non-working poor than with labor-union bureaucracy; more attuned to the Negro's need for participation and pride in his blackness than to the old slogans of integration.' "

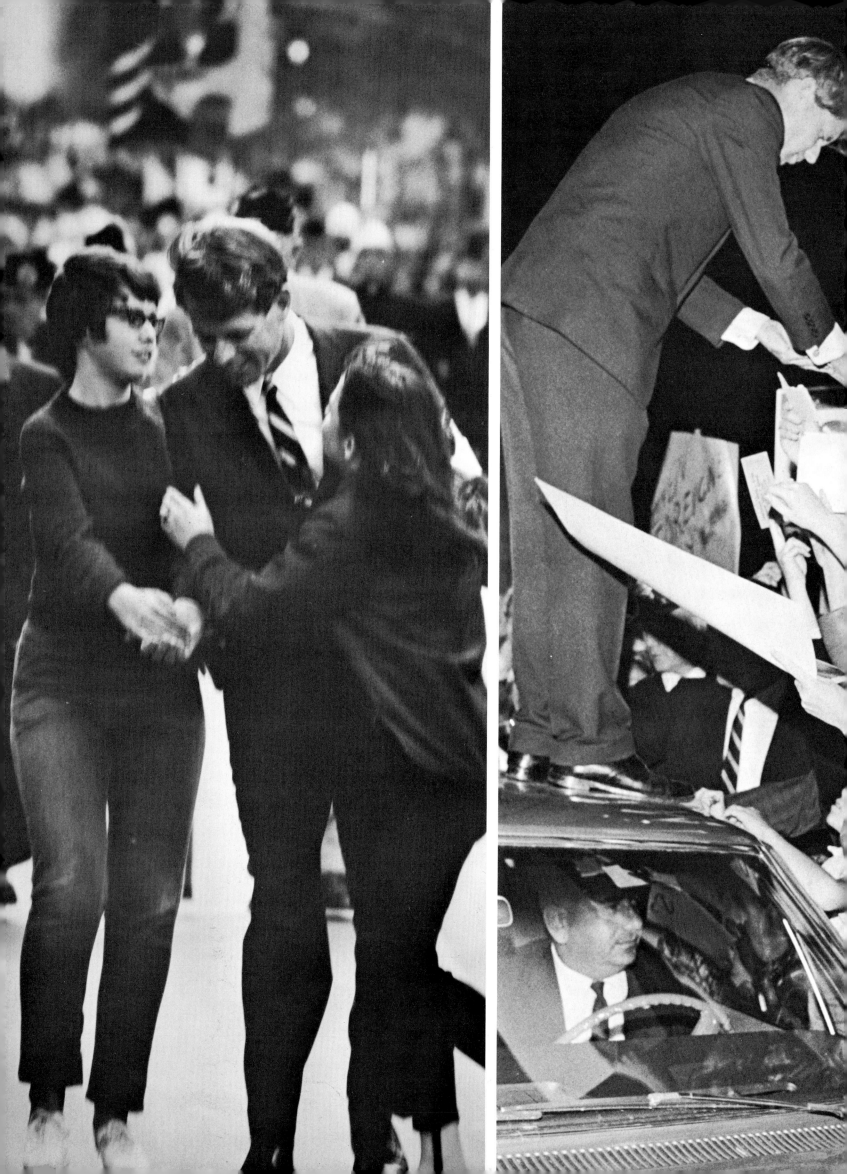

If his displays of warmth seem spontaneous, his displays of arrogance seem similarly natural. His arrogance is not vicious, not premeditated; it is the milder arrogance of wealth and position, and it reveals itself in small ways. Some of it is amusing—his habit of roaming without money, borrowing subway fare and church donations from reporters and aides—but some of it is not. Generally, he does not open doors; others open doors for him. He does not carry his own attaché case; someone plucks it from his hand and carries it for him. He does not wait for people; passengers aboard his family's private plane, *The Caroline*, are told

(above) "The best explanation seems to be that Bobby Kennedy quotes his brother the way a good preacher quotes the Bible. It is his favorite, most dependable text."
(opposite page, above) Cuzco, Peru, 1965. (below) South Africa, 1966. "Certainly, the legacy-legend of J.F.K. lends itself to Bobby Kennedy's charisma. And, certainly, he encourages the connection . . ."

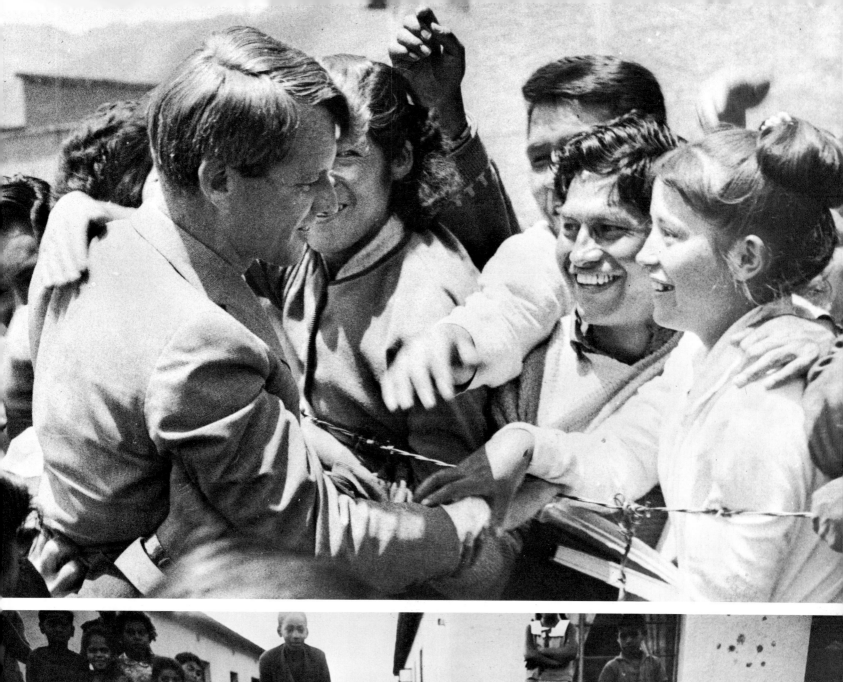

William Manchester, author of
The Death of a President.
"Everything turned into a
nightmare."

that the aircraft takes off when he boards, and if they are tardy, they lose their ride. Anyone less accustomed to being waited upon—and many equally accustomed—would either feel embarrassed by the excessive attention or would have to demand it. Kennedy is not embarrassed, which would be winsome, and he is not demanding, which would be repellent; he is accepting, which is merely irritating.

His puritanical strain, bordering on the self-righteous, can be irritating too. He gives the impression that he firmly believes in good and evil, in saints and sinners—which would be fine if he would only allow for a touch of evil, a touch of the sinner, in himself. But he seems to have utter faith in himself, complete trust in his own morality. Yet he has the saving ability to kid his own puritanism. "It isn't that I'm a saint," he told one reporter. "It's just that I've never found it necessary to be a sinner."

His sense of humor saves him often. It is a dry and pointed sense of humor, and usually, even while it is pointed at himself, it serves, deliberately, to blunt critics' charges against him.

One morning, before leaving his home for his office, he carried *The New York Times* upstairs to his wife, then hurried downstairs, turned to a friend, and said, "That's my good deed for the day. Now I can go back to being ruthless."

When a biographer of John Kennedy wrote that Bobby was anti-Semitic, Ed Guthman, the Attorney General's press secretary, who is Jewish, brought the book to his boss and pointed out the indictment. Kennedy stared hard at Guthman. "I always knew," he said, deadpan, "there was something about you I hated."

During the 1964 senatorial campaign, after discussing with his staff the meager assistance he was getting from the New York State Democratic Committee, he said, "I guess I shouldn't complain. If they were any good, I wouldn't be here, would I?"

In 1967, at a dinner in Philadelphia of the Americans for Democratic Action, he spotted Congressman William Green, whose father had been a political boss in the tradition the ADA was born to oppose. "Billy," said Kennedy from the

speaker's rostrum, "how would your father feel if he knew you were here?" Pause. "Come to think of it, how would *my* father feel if he knew *I* was here?"

"The cost of campaigning has become so high," he told a college audience in 1967, "that to make a candidate and his views well known in a state like California or New York is impossible without either a well-known personality or enormous sums of money." Pause. "As an unknown virtually without funds, I was, of course, an exception."

And, during a question-and-answer period following the same speech, when a student pressed him about his days with McCarthy, his notes slipped off the rostrum and, as he bent down, he said, "I'm not disappearing. I'm just picking up my notes." The ensuing laughter almost drowned out his evasive answer: "Well, I found it very interesting."

Kennedy uses humor to cover his lapses as well as his past. Once, when he was Attorney General, he gave a welcoming speech at a Belafonte concert sponsored by the Foreign Student Service Council. "You people," said Kennedy, "are exemplifying what my brother meant when he said in his inaugural address, 'Ask what you can do for — uh — do not ask what you can do — uh — ask not what you can do for your country but . . .' well, anyhow, you remember his words." The audience began to laugh, and Kennedy, reddening, shrugged. "That's why my *brother* is President," he said.

Critics charge, with varying degrees of intensity, that if John F. Kennedy brought intelligence to the Presidency, Robert F. Kennedy would not. Certainly, as a student, he never threatened to join Phi Beta Kappa, and as a young man, his thirst for knowledge seemed quenched much more easily by facts than by comprehension. Even as the thirst grew, Bobby Kennedy suffered in comparison with his brother.

"Jack travels in that speculative area where doubt lives," Charles F. Spalding, a family friend, once said. "Bobby does not travel there."

"Bobby is considerably more primitive toward ideas, people, and institutions

(left) Pierre Salinger recommended and first contacted Manchester. (center) Burke Marshall helped draw up the Kennedy-Manchester agreement, and then represented the Kennedy's during The Affair. (right) John Seigenthaler, former Justice Department aide and now editor of The Nashville Tennessean, read and screened the Manchester manuscript (along with Ed Guthman) for Kennedy.

67

Both Frank Mankiewicz and Ed Guthman felt they "let Bob down on this book." Mankiewicz is quietly, if wittily, determined not to let anything remotely similar happen again.

than his brother," said an official serving the Kennedy Administration. "He doesn't have the literary background or interests the President does." But the official saw hope. "Bobby has a limited, but growing, acquaintance with intellectualism," he said. "The more he is exposed, the more he is impressed."

In the eyes of his friends, not surprisingly, the promise of Kennedy's intelligence has been fulfilled. "He is certainly not an intellectual," says Robert Morgenthau, "but he has an ability to get down to the guts of the problem."

"He is not scholarly at all," says Peter Edelman. "He is instinctive. He sees to the essence of things. He finds the one thing that cuts to the heart of the matter."

Adam Walinsky cites two samples of the Kennedy intelligence, both involving his testimony before a congressional committee studying a new immigration bill Walinsky had helped draft in the Justice Department. "Mr. Attorney General," said a Republican congressman, straying from the subject, "some people are

Jacqueline Kennedy entering a law office with Dick Goodwin and Simon Rifkind during the height of The Affair, where for the first time she forced herself to read the book closely. Goodwin began as a friend and neighbor of Manchester's. This relationship — like so many others — was eroded during the battle.

saying we should discontinue aid to Vietnam. Isn't this aid and comfort to the enemy? Couldn't they be prosecuted under the sedition laws?"

Kennedy thought, then said, "Well, congressman, that's a very important statute, but it seems to me it should be interpreted very narrowly." Kennedy considered further. Republicans had been attacking the Democratic Administration for failing to provide proper aircraft and equipment for the American soldiers in Vietnam. Kennedy mentioned the criticism. "That could be interpreted as aid and comfort to the enemy too," he said.

"It never occurred to me," says Walinsky, who prides himself on thinking of everything. "It was the perfect answer."

After the testimony, Walinsky, who had also been questioned, was assigned to go over the remarks of Justice Department witnesses and edit them for the hearing record, a standard practice. "Kennedy speaks in short, simple sentences," Walinsky says. "Most people who consider themselves intellectuals tend to come up with long sentences with a lot of dependent clauses. When I read the testimony, I found I had to correct his much less than mine and others. His spoken English was much closer to written English."

The most acceptable theory is that Bobby Kennedy is learning, out of necessity and out of desire. "One of his first liberal friends, William O. Douglas [noted] his 'unique capacity for growth,'" wrote Arthur Schlesinger Jr. "Thus at some point Robert Kennedy grew aware of the world of mind and sensibility in which his brother had been so long at ease; and he determined to explore this world for himself."

Schlesinger went further, to suggest that Kennedy had begun immersing himself in concerts and ballet, even though Ethel Kennedy has explained that neither she nor her husband has any appreciation of music, and to suggest that Kennedy

Kennedy twice tried unsuccessfully to separate himself geographically, if not actually to disassociate himself, from Jacqueline Kennedy's attitudes and eventual law suit. Here he is skiing at Sun Valley, Idaho, shortly before Christmas, 1966.

69

has turned into a hungry reader, stressing history and biography. His friends repeatedly claim that Kennedy is an avid reader, that he reads for broad knowledge, not just for specific facts; and, when he is traveling, he often sticks a book under his arm. The book, however, is seldom opened, at least not in the presence of reporters.

The less charitable anti-Bobby voices weight their case against his intelligence with one curious bit of ammunition. Someone once revealed that Kennedy listens to recordings of Shakespeare in the shower; the critics argue that this demonstrates, beyond contradiction, his intellectual shortcomings. The argument is not persuasive; Shakespeare, in the shower or the Old Vic, has never hurt anyone's capacity to think. It is surely more stimulating than listening to the hiss of the shower nozzle, or even to country music.

And, apparently, Kennedy listens in the shower. He once spent an evening in Rome with the Richard Burtons, and when the Welsh actor recited the St. Crispin's Day speech from *Henry V*, Kennedy caught him in a slight misquotation. Burton insisted he was right; Kennedy insisted he was right; the actor lost the case.

From a limited inventory of Bobby Kennedy's characteristics, a picture emerges of an interesting man, even an impressive man, but not an extraordinary man. He is at least reasonably intelligent; he has a quick sense of humor, a firm sense of morality, a frustrating mixture of arrogance and compassion. These are private traits, and in most men, they would have an impact only on a small sphere. But Bobby Kennedy is not a private man. He is a public man. What sets him apart, what makes him extraordinary, is his dedication to, or obsession with, the twin fields of politics and power. They cannot be separated; almost by definition, a politician is a man in search of power, and how he acquires that power, how he uses it, and how he reacts to it determine the sort of politician he is.

Kennedy, of course, seeks power, the ultimate power of the Presidency. Totally apart from the value of his ideas, apart from the depth of his belief in them, Kennedy wants to win. His fierce competitiveness, instilled at home, conditioned in sports, and polished in politics, is so obvious it is accepted even by his enemies. "Bobby Kennedy has a tremendous will to win," Richard Nixon once said, not without admiration. Once Kennedy wanted to win primarily for the sake of winning; that spirit persists, but merged with it now, to an extent that defies precise measurement, is a conviction that his victory is important beyond himself. Others, prejudiced by their closeness to him, share this conviction. "The kind of guy you want for President," says Joe Dolan, Kennedy's administrative assistant, "is the guy you shake in the middle of the night, when the radar blips are going wild and the transatlantic cables are cut, and the guy acts better, tougher than ever. John F. Kennedy was that guy. So is Robert Kennedy."

Bobby Kennedy's approach to power appears to have shifted with his motivation. He used to be incredibly blunt. "Bobby is more direct than Jack," their father, Joseph P. Kennedy Sr., once said. "Jack has always been one to persuade people to do things. Bobby tends to tell people what to do. He resembles me much more than any of the other children. I make up my mind quickly and go ahead and get it

Kennedy's second flight from The Battle of the Book occurred in January, 1967, when he traveled to Europe. Here he, and another fellow traveler, William vanden Heuvel, are shown surrounded by newsmen at the Elysée Palace in Paris after Kennedy met with French President Charles de Gaulle. Also, in Paris, Kennedy either did or did not receive a peace feeler from a North Vietnamese envoy, provoking both Lyndon Johnson and more unfavorable publicity. During this period, Kennedy's immense popularity slipped. He has not yet recovered fully.

done. Bobby is the same way." Similarly, but more mildly, Bobby himself explained, "I don't ask myself these questions about motives or ambition or why I did something. I get the job done."

Now he seems to have softened. "He was a pusher, a shover," says a Boston newspaperman who has known Bobby Kennedy for fifteen years. "He isn't any more."

Friends attribute the softening to maturity, which is only one explanation. A second is that Bobby Kennedy, consciously or unconsciously, as he looks upon himself increasingly as the heir to his brother's ideals, tries to act more like his brother. And a third explanation is that he does not use power so rawly these days simply because he lacks the raw power he once had. When his brother was President, Bobby Kennedy was the second most powerful man in the government. Now he is only a senator, a senator often at odds with the Administration, and his power is barely a shadow of what it was.

When Kennedy had power, he did not waste it. He refused to tolerate laziness or ineptitude, he destroyed egos and bruised people's lives, but he drove himself hard, and he managed his jobs well. He was, on balance, an excellent campaign manager for his brother, an excellent Attorney General for his brother.

His reaction to power, when he had it, was not, despite his harshest critics, particularly unpleasant. He never seemed overly impressed with his own importance. Perhaps more disturbing than anything else was his self-righteousness about power. "We hire people for their ability, not their race," Kennedy once insisted to a group of civil-rights pickets at the Justice Department. He stocked his

71

voice with holiness, and, at the same time, he and his brother occasionally stocked the Administration, in judges and even in Cabinet members, with expediency.

It is difficult to gauge exactly how the Bobby Kennedy of today would employ and react to great power. He has been away from it since the assassination. Certainly, he drives his own staff sternly, but the staff seems to relish it. Certainly, his reaction to the loss of power is a discernible longing for it. But Bobby Kennedy can best be judged today only by his search for power, his techniques for acquiring power.

The emphasis is on the package, the proper combination of stance and substance. He is a thoroughly modern politician, and he knows, perhaps better than any other politician, how to use the modern system of mass communications to project himself most favorably upon the public. Even as he criticizes the system to college audiences, he employs it to its fullest. "I think a person must be out of his mind if he thinks he can manage news," Bobby Kennedy once told *U. S. News & World Report.* By his own definition, Bobby Kennedy is crazy like a fox; he not only thinks he can manage news, he does. In its thrust, if not its effect, his orchestration of the Vietnam speech was worthy of a virtuoso. Build the greatest audience for the greatest impact. Build to a crescendo.

Bobby Kennedy is out to seduce the press. As seducers go, his intentions are honorable, and Andrew Glass of *The Washington Post* points out that "Kennedy is as wooed as he is wooing." He is a potential President, and reporters, just like legislators, lobbyists, and social climbers, want to be close to a potential President. A majority of the press, even men whose jobs depend on a reasonable relationship with Lyndon Johnson, want to be loved, or at least courted, by Kennedy. The feeling is requited. Glass, accompanying Kennedy on a South American tour, reported, "All along, the senator's official press secretary . . . was sending [him] reports on how the television film clips and news stories were being 'played.' [He] was upset, because—back home—the clippings were scanty and the 'play' subdued."

(above) Two views of the crowded, frenetic Kennedy outer offices in the Senate Office Building in Washington. At left, Angie Novello, Frank Mankiewicz and two secretaries. At right, Adam Walinsky and Peter Edelman. (left) In the maelstrom, Joe Dolan runs a remarkably efficient office.

Kennedy studies the press and reacts to it. He is not a bleeder; although he can be almost vicious in blaming subordinates for unfavorable stories, he does not brood about criticism in print. More often, he dismisses attacks with humor ("I'm not *that* bad") or with contempt (of one critic, he says, "He's a woman"). But, just as he and his staff maneuver to get complimentary stories published, they

"The Kennedy Corner" of Robert Kennedy's private office is devoted to the memory of John F. Kennedy, and other members of the family. "Among the family, Bobby depends heavily upon Stephen Smith, his brother-in-law, who manages the Kennedy enterprises and managed both brothers' senatorial campaigns." (below) the entrance to Kennedy's New York City office.

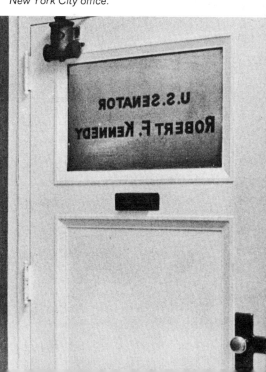

Joseph Kraft, a liberal, intellectual, journalist, and author, is thought to be a particularly influential member of the informal R.F.K. brain trust.

apply pressure to stifle damaging stories. During a California trip in 1966, he heard that a reporter was preparing a less-than-flattering story, and promptly, in front of perhaps twenty other newspapermen, he accused the reporter of "sensationalism." For emphasis, he had an aide telephone the reporter's editor and complain.

In 1967, when a Washington television station called Kennedy's office and asked for his cooperation on a special program, the senator's press secretary spent nearly ten minutes telling the caller how cruelly unfair the station's anti-Bobby editorials had been. "Why should we cooperate with you?" the press secretary demanded.

The press, despite its natural and practical affinity for Kennedy, resents his manipulations, resents being conned. One reporter, friendly to Kennedy, was incensed by an article appearing in a monthly magazine, bylined by Robert F. Kennedy Jr., analyzing "my father, the senator." "He demands family privacy," the reporter snapped, "but he thinks nothing of prostituting his own son. He wants everything both ways."

Kennedy's most unnerving, possibly disastrous, brush with managing the news grew out of William Manchester's book, *The Death of a President*. The Kennedy family, principally Bobby and his brother's widow, in effect commissioned Manchester to write the story of the assassination. They sat for his interviews, withheld their cooperation from anyone else, and insisted he submit his manuscript for their review. Examined in its best light, the situation was this: The Kennedys found it painful to discuss the assassination, and they found it unfair to history to suppress the details. They decided to select a responsible writer, bestow all their knowledge upon him, and present, through him, a factual and insightful picture of the assassination. They sought to check his manuscript only to guarantee accuracy of fact and insight.

Everything turned into a nightmare. The Kennedys erred in demanding the right to review a writer's work; if they trusted him enough to choose him, they should have trusted his intelligence and art. Manchester erred in agreeing to the review; he should have fought for his autonomy. The situation degenerated into bitterness, involving book publishers, magazine publishers, and lawyers, and, in the end, Bobby Kennedy came out looking the worst. He came out looking like a censor, like a manipulator, like a man capable of exerting cruel pressures. And he was. He stained his image badly. Probably no other single R.F.K. episode antagonized so many people.

"If anyone had told me the project was going to turn out the way it did," says Ed Guthman, Kennedy's former press secretary, "I never would have believed him." Guthman, now national editor of *The Los Angeles Times*, and John Seigenthaler, a former aide who is now editor of *The Nashville Tennessean*, were Kennedy's choice to read and screen the Manchester manuscript. "Newspapermen have a knack for being able to spot trouble," Guthman says. "I feel we let Bob down on this book. There was a red flag waving all the way down the track and we never spotted it."

Perhaps Kennedy never wanted to get involved with the book. Perhaps Jacqueline Kennedy prodded him into carrying the fight against publication of parts of

"No real cabinet exists — 'unless,' says John Kenneth Galbraith, 'this cabinet is a thing of such singular originality that it never meets and never discusses anything' — but the men are available."

75

the manuscript. Perhaps he honestly believed that Manchester had violated his trust, that the feelings of the President's widow had to be protected. Whatever his motivations, Kennedy, personally and through his representatives, antagonized the publishers, alienated Manchester, and emerged, fairly or unfairly, the prime villain, looking at best like a man suppressing history, at worst like a man distorting history, trying to use the book as a weapon in his feud with Lyndon Johnson. Bobby Kennedy found himself hopelessly trapped among contradictions that tasted like lies.

Kennedy himself is not a liar—"much less than most politicians," suggests a Washington reporter—but, unfortunately, he is often surrounded by lies. Associates lie for him—about little things. For instance, when Kennedy is flying first-class, an aide, fearful that Kennedy might look like a rich man, tells a reporter the senator is flying tourist. When the reporter sees Kennedy in first class, he looks worse than rich. Or an aide, after working all night on a task for Kennedy, claims to have had several hours of sleep, fearful that Kennedy might look like a martinet. When Kennedy himself mentions that the aide was up all the night, the whole operation becomes suspect.

The little lies, so stupid and unnecessary, are most harmful because they encourage the possibility of a big lie, a lie about the depth and integrity of Kennedy's political philosophy, an area still vulnerable to doubt. His posture is generally, if not predictably, liberal. Once, at an ADA banquet, he attributed his liberalism simply to debates with Arthur Schlesinger Jr.: "He won and I am here."

His supporters equate Bobby Kennedy's conversion to liberalism with his brother's. "Some people have their liberalism 'made' by the time they reach their late twenties," John F. Kennedy told biographer James MacGregor Burns. "I didn't. I was caught in crosscurrents and eddies. It was only later that I got into the stream of things."

If Kennedy's concern with liberal causes is now beyond dispute, his sincerity is still debated. Even ignoring the past—when he jumped from one side of the wiretapping controversy to the other, when he leaped from unawareness of civil rights to total commitment—he is still suspect. One of his senatorial staffers once researched existing housing legislation and learned that New York City could get $8,000,000 from the federal government to improve housing. The city was not getting the money, and the staff member urged Kennedy to request it. "Why should I help Lindsay?" he responded. His instinct, in that case, was not to help New York Mayor John Lindsay, a political rival. "When he talks about helping poor people," says a former Kennedy aide, "you wonder if he means it."

Yet most of the indications are that he does mean it, that he does want to eliminate poverty, that he does seek peace, that he is concerned with human dignity. The possibility remains that he turned to liberalism as an expedient and genuinely liked what he found. "What encourages me most about Bobby," says Joseph Rauh, one of the major voices of liberalism, "is that he should think liberalism is the wave of the future."

One indication of Kennedy's sincerity is that he takes stands he could avoid,

77

"The ties of family remain strong among the Kennedys, and Bobby obviously turns to Teddy for company and friendship, if not advice."

"He is utterly devoted to his wife, Ethel, a wonderfully unaffected woman, as friendly, cheerful, and likable as she is athletic."

stands, like the Vietnam speech, that could hurt more than help him. "Kennedy is opting more and more for the high-risk, high-gain issue," wrote Andrew Kopkind in *The New Republic*. "Nothing in the book of common political practice demands that he approve of blood donations for the Viet Cong, that he champion the grapestrikers' cause, that he criticize the Justice Department's refusal to allow burial of a Communist in Arlington cemetary. . . . Yet he has done all those things."

Kopkind theorized persuasively that Kennedy is not directing his appeal at any standard large group of voters, that he is not seeking to capture any identifiable bloc, that he is, if anything, only loosely shaping the outlines of an organization that could be called a "Kennedy Party."

The Kennedy Party exists—not formally, not permanently, not as a threat to the established political parties. It is a group of men and ideas united by resistance to the direction of the Johnson Administration. The party is vague, but its core is specific: Kennedy, his staff, and his brain trust—men inherited from his brother and men gathered in his own career who contribute to his thinking.

Kennedy's staff is not quite like any other senator's, probably because Kennedy is not quite like any other senator. Unlike any of his colleagues, including former governors, he considers the Senate a demotion. He uses the Senate as a sounding board and a staging area, a convenient arena for the testing of ideas, the making of speeches, and the accumulation of support. But he has no plans to devote his life to making the laws of the land, and he knows this, his fellow senators know it, and his staff knows it.

Perhaps the scope of Kennedy's ambition makes it easier for his staff to accept the working conditions. He drives them furiously ("You learn to swing with it or you leave," says one staffer), and ten-hour days and weekend assignments are standard. Sometimes he loses his temper and explodes at a member of the staff ("When you do something wrong, he lets you know"); and often he will assign two or more people to the same project without telling each what the others are doing. Every level of the senator's staff operates under pressure—from his top aides, who must be ready to face every conceivable issue, to his clerks, who must record and reply to nearly a thousand letters a day, to his receptionists, who are besieged by phone calls and visitors. Yet almost everyone seems to thrive under the pressure; the surface reactions are enjoyment and loyalty. Just as in practically every phase of his personality, Kennedy, in his dealings with his staff, has at least two sides. He shows his appreciation for their efforts. He arranges for his staff to escape from duty to attend his major speeches. He gives monthly beer-and-Coke parties in his office and invites the entire staff. For Christmas, 1966, he presented each female employee with a gold loyalty pill, engraved "R.F.K." on one side and "Loyal" on the other.

The Hatch River expedition, one of the many recent Kennedy family explorations of the good life.

The members of his staff are somewhat surprising, not what one would expect. "He should have been a movie director," says Frank Mankiewicz, the nephew of movie producer Joseph Mankiewicz. "He casts against type."

Besides Mankiewicz, the key members of the Washington staff are legislative aides Walinsky, Edelman, and Pigman, administrative aide Dolan, and personal secretary Angie Novello. They range in age from their early thirties (Walinsky and Edelman) to middle forties (Dolan). All the men except Pigman graduated from law school.

Walinsky, a New Yorker out of Yale Law, a gifted speechwriter and tireless researcher, is intellectual and intense in equal measure. He thinks so highly of his own ability that in 1965, before he turned thirty, he offered to run for mayor of New York City to save the city and the Democratic Party. He thinks so highly of Kennedy's ability that he concedes the senator is smarter than he; Walinsky can praise no more. His mod shirts and flowing black hair have prompted one senator to label him a "beatnik"; his abruptness and absorption in his work have prompted others to label him arrogant. He is arrogant at times, but he is also bright, thoughtful, and playful: He once told Kennedy that he would cut his hair if the senator would take a political stand he favored.

Edelman, a Minnesotan out of Harvard Law, clerked for Supreme Court Justice Arthur Goldberg, then served with Walinsky in the Justice Department. More composed than Walinsky, he seems equally intelligent.

Both young men were buried deep in the Justice Department, left it to work on Kennedy's senatorial campaign, and impressed the candidate enough to earn their present jobs. They handle most of the work on the glamorous issues; Pigman, a political scientist, backs them up.

Mankiewicz was a Peace Corps administrator concerned with South America when he met Kennedy. Although he had a degree in journalism, as well as in law, he had not worked in the field for more than fifteen years. When Kennedy offered him the post of press secretary, Mankiewicz reasoned, "Either he's researched me very well or he's willing to gamble. Either way, that's pretty good." He took the job in 1966 with little knowledge of press relations; he gets along well with the press now by being helpful and by being amusing. He still has a touch of Hollywood in him, and he contributes some of the best wisecracks to the Kennedy speeches.

Dolan, in contrast, is staid. A native New Yorker, via Denver, he talks and acts like an administrator. He runs an efficient office, winces at some of Mankiewicz's irreverent jokes, and hopes, eventually, to return to his law practice in Colorado.

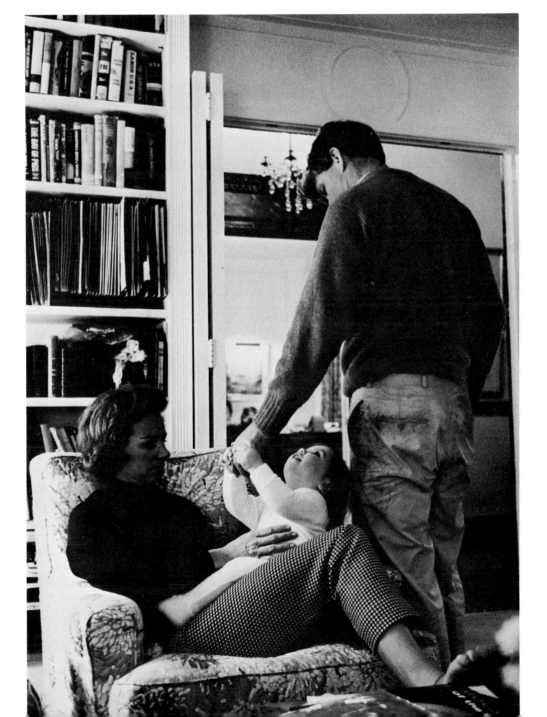

" 'I'd die if I made a girl cry. I don't think I've ever made my wife cry.' "

R. F. K.

Angie Novello, Kennedy's secretary since 1957, is professionally possessive about her boss, carefully screens who sees him and who speaks to him. Easygoing with outsiders, stern with her subordinates, she has traveled with the Kennedy family to Europe, Asia, South America, and Africa, but her view of the world is limited. She spent most of her time on each trip sitting in a hotel room typing.

The official Kennedy staff—Tom Johnston, a former television producer, runs the New York City office, and Jerry Bruno, a veteran political organizer, runs the upstate New York office—shares Kennedy's attention and interest with his unofficial staff. The brain trust includes, in part, Goodwin, Schlesinger, Sorensen, Guthman, Seigenthaler, vanden Heuvel, Pierre Salinger (once John Kennedy's press secretary), Burke Marshall (once chief of the Justice Department's civil-rights section), John J. Burns (the New York State Democratic chairman), a handful of journalists, notably Joseph Kraft, several former members of the Kennedy Administration now based at Harvard's John F. Kennedy School of Government, and several members of the Johnson Administration, who are expert at discretion. Carter Burden, one of New York society's "beautiful people," lends his special

tone to Kennedy's Manhattan office. Hundreds of friends and acquaintances Bobby has made since college days occasionally volunteer information and assistance.

Both staffs—official and unofficial—couple fierce pride in Kennedy with a sensitivity that borders on paranoia. If a single story unfavorable to Kennedy appears in, say, *Newsweek*, one of the inner circle is certain to ask, "Why is *Newsweek* against us?" The inner circle, even more than the senator, tends to divide the world into pro-Bobby and anti-Bobby camps. Occasionally, the sense of combat gives way to humor. When a reporter noticed a Kennedy aide sitting at his desk reading *Lyndon B. Johnson: The Exercise of Power*, the aide grinned and said, "Know thy enemy."

Kennedy's Washington aides, incidentally, take an almost cruel pleasure in minimizing the abilities of the senator's younger brother. Some openly poke fun at Teddy Kennedy's intelligence; members of Teddy's staff, in turn, point out that Bobby has difficulty finding the Senate chamber.

The two brothers kid each other too, but their kidding seems more good-

natured than that of their subordinates. The ties of family remain strong among the Kennedys, and Bobby obviously turns to Teddy for company and friendship, if not advice. Among the family, Bobby depends heavily upon Stephen Smith, his brother-in-law, who manages the Kennedy enterprises and managed both brothers' senatorial campaigns. Bobby Kennedy is not so close to another brother-in-law, Sargent Shriver, who runs Lyndon Johnson's poverty program. Kennedy and Shriver do not openly feud, but they needle each other, and some of the needles draw blood.

Kennedy's relationship with his immediate family, like the rest of his life, is open to varying interpretations. Relaxing at Hickory Hill, he can be the ideal father, romping on the lawn with any of the ten children (Douglas Harriman Kennedy joined the clan March 24, 1967), encouraging them in school and in hobbies, drawing them into the frequent touch-football games. Kennedy at his family best is Kennedy watching the Super Bowl on television in his den, wrestling on the floor with one of his daughters, dropping an ice cube, for a joke, down her back. He is utterly devoted to his wife, Ethel, a wonderfully unaffected woman, as friendly, cheerful, and likable as she is athletic. When Kennedy toured Europe in January, 1967, he sent his wife a telegram every day, always the same fond message, always in the language of the country he was visiting. Fortunately for Ethel Kennedy, the first message came from London.

Yet often Kennedy is away from his family, and often he seems completely unaware of what is happening with them. His wife shields him from knowledge of both the children's illnesses and her own. Once, the day after Ethel Kennedy postponed an interview with a reporter because she was sick, Bobby Kennedy approached the reporter and asked, "Did you see Ethel yesterday?" Apparently, no one had told him that his wife had been ill.

"I'm wondering how often you make your wife cry," a female journalist said to him one day, and the comment puzzled him. "I'd die if I made a girl cry," he said. "I don't think I've ever made my wife cry." He believed it. Bobby Kennedy, quite likely, often believes what he wants to believe.

This is a complex man, full of strengths and weaknesses, full of virtues and faults—which puts him among the majority. Yet his flaws are human, if annoying, and they seem more than matched by his energy, his awareness, his understanding. He has already lived a vigorously full life, through a competitive childhood, through an apprenticeship as an investigator, through an education in political campaigns, through enlightenment as Attorney General. Now he is a senator, and he wants to rise higher. The ultimate question is one of trust. If Bobby Kennedy is, as he says, honestly dedicated to public service, if he is a man changed by experience and not by expediency, his warmest admirers are justified. But if he is all package and no product, if he is insincere, he is the perpetrator of a terrible crime, and his severest critics are justified.

The balance leans perceptibly, but not completely, toward trust.

CHAPTER FOUR

UP
FROM
RICHES

The potatoes turned black, and famine swept Ireland, and in 1848, Patrick Kennedy huddled in the dank steerage of a miserable ship and sailed to East Boston to found the Kennedy clan of the United States. One of Bobby Kennedy's grandfathers—Patrick Kennedy's son—was a saloonkeeper; the other was born in a tenement. The Horatio Alger aspect of Bobby Kennedy's life ends right there.

The saloonkeeper sired Joseph Patrick Kennedy, Bobby's father, a Harvard graduate who was president of a bank at the age of twenty-five and a multimillionaire before he reached forty; and the man born in a tenement, John F. Fitzgerald, became "Honey Fitz," the mayor of Boston, and sired Rose Fitzgerald, Bobby's mother. Robert Francis Kennedy was born November 20, 1925, in Brookline, Massachusetts, the seventh of Rose and Joseph Kennedy's nine children, the third of four boys, the runt of the litter. Before his first birthday, Bobby Kennedy moved, with his family and its servants, to Riverdale, a suburb of New York City. They moved in a private railroad car. Bobby Kennedy has traveled well ever since.

Bobby Kennedy grew up in the Depression, and, like so many other children of the time, he sold magazines, *The Saturday Evening Post* and the *Ladies' Home Journal*, door-to-door. But not so many other children moved door-to-door in a chauffeur-driven Rolls-Royce. This is, equally, a fine measure of Bobby Kennedy's childhood and a fine measure of Joseph Kennedy's financial skill. Through hard work and a fierce shrewdness, Joe Kennedy accumulated a fortune in the stock market, in real estate, and in the movie business, and he did not surrender his fortune to the Depression. He did, before the market crashed, surrender his home in Riverdale; the Kennedys weathered the Depression in a $250,000 Georgian mansion in nearby, but more exclusive, Bronxville.

The three principal influences on young Bobby were his father, his mother, and his oldest brother, Joseph Kennedy Jr. The father bestowed upon him an overwhelming desire for victory and power, an awareness of politics, and, not least, a

R.F.K.

Kennedy family portrait taken in 1934. Left to right: Edward, Jean, Robert, Patricia, Eunice, Kathleen, Rosemary, John, Rose Kennedy, and Joseph P. Kennedy.

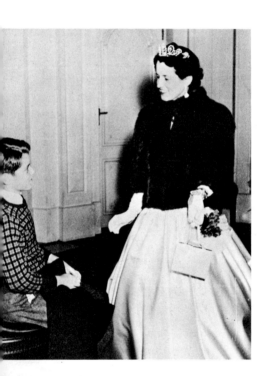

trust fund that eventually grew to more than $10,000,000. Joe Kennedy gave each of his children the same gifts, of money and of personality. "I put them in a position," he once said, "where each one of them could spit in my eye and tell me where to go. And there was nothing to prevent them from becoming rich idle bums if they wanted to."

Joe Kennedy was often an absentee father—he spent considerable time in Hollywood and later, working for Franklin Roosevelt on the Securities and Exchange Commission, in Washington—but his impact could not have been greater if he had never left the house. "His personality was so strong, his ideas so definite, his views and outlook so determined, that he dominated our home and our lives," Bobby Kennedy later reminisced.

Rose Kennedy coped with the children. "I handled general management as well as being in charge of production," she said. To each of her children, she gave a strong sense of family that persists ("If I had known it was going to be a contest," she said, when Bobby's tenth child was born, "I wouldn't have stopped at nine"), an understanding that other people were less fortunate ("Their father and I always tried to impress on them that they had an obligation, that when you are

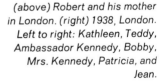

(above) Robert and his mother in London. (right) 1938, London. Left to right: Kathleen, Teddy, Ambassador Kennedy, Bobby, Mrs. Kennedy, Patricia, and Jean.

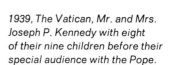

1939, The Vatican, Mr. and Mrs.
Joseph P. Kennedy with eight
of their nine children before their
special audience with the Pope.

given more, more is expected of you''), and deep religious conviction. Rose
Kennedy attended Mass each morning, listened to her children's prayers each
night and to their catechism lessons each Friday. "Bobby was always very devout,"
she once said, "probably the most devout of all the children."

Deliberately, Rose Kennedy concentrated her attention upon the older children.
"You start the older ones up right," she explained, "and the younger children
will follow along."

The oldest of the boys, Joe Jr., was a natural leader, and he offered a model for
both Jack, two years younger than he, and Bobby, eight years younger than Jack.
Joe and Jack, so close in age, fell into a natural rivalry, but the relationship of Joe
and Bobby was strictly teacher and pupil. Young Joe—and his father, when he
joined the family either in Bronxville or, more often, in Hyannis Port—taught
Bobby to sail, to grip a football, to play tennis, to ski; he fired the competitive
instincts in Bobby, and he fired them well. Slighter and shorter than his brothers
had been, Bobby early began to compensate with rugged enthusiasm. He was
always wiry, persistent, combative, proud, and he showed the same lack of fear
of injury that marks his own children (who pose for family portraits, regularly,
in splints and bandages).

Once, playing in a toolshed, he overturned an old radiator which tumbled onto
his foot, breaking a toe. For almost half an hour, rather than confess his clumsi-
ness to his mother, he kept the shoe on his foot. Finally, he exposed his wound,
and his mother, who knew when to discipline him and when to salve him, sent
him to the doctor.

(above) One of Robert
Kennedy's favorite pictures,
taken in 1938 at the Tower of
London. Seen are Teddy, Bobby,
and Jean. (left) This picture was
taken in Boston in 1939. Left to
right: Joseph P. Kennedy, Jr.,
Joseph P. Kennedy, Sr., Robert
F. Kennedy, and John F. Kennedy.

(right) 1941, the Kennedy estate at Palm Beach, Florida. Left to right: Eunice, Bobby, Teddy, and Jean. (below) 1943. At 17, Robert Kennedy is sworn into the Navy as an Aviation Cadet while his father looks on.

(above) In the Navy. (right) The Milton-Groton game, 1942. Carrying the ball is Dave Hackett, still a close friend. Blocking is Bob Kennedy.

Another time, when his sister Eunice tossed chocolate icing at him, he chased her through the house until he trapped her in front of a table. Like a bull, Bobby lowered his head and charged. Like a matador, Eunice stepped aside. Bobby cracked his head into the table, opening a sizable cut, and once more went off to the doctor.

His interests ran, like most boys', to sports and pets—he kept white rabbits, who multiplied, and a pig named Porky, who didn't—and his interest in school ran far behind. "Bobby didn't read very much when he was young," his mother later recalled. "He was one of the ones I had to keep urging to read." His grades were never exceptional, but he did attend excellent schools, many of them, starting with the public schools in Bronxville.

When Bobby was twelve, President Roosevelt named his father Ambassador to the Court of St. James's, and Joseph Kennedy, who became a popular Irishman among the English, moved his family to London. Bobby finished his elementary education at the Gibbs School, where he added cricket and soccer to his games, attended parties with Princess Margaret and Princess Elizabeth, and joined the British Boy Scouts (only on the condition that he did not have to swear allegiance to the king).

The family had a tour of Europe and a glimpse of Nazi Germany before Joseph Kennedy, in 1940, resigned as ambassador. Attacked by American liberals for isolationism, appeasement, and hints of anti-Semitism, Joseph Kennedy announced he would devote himself to keeping the United States out of the war.

ROBERT FRANCIS KENNEDY
Born November 20, 1925, in Brookline, Massachusetts. Prepared at Milton Academy. Entered Harvard as a Freshman in March, 1944. Home Address: Marchand Ave., Hyannisport, Massachusetts. Winthrop House. Informal Freshman Football (Captain, 1944); Varsity Football; Informal Lacrosse; Informal Rugby; Winthrop House Swimming; Winthrop House Committee; Catholic Club; Hasty Pudding-Institute of 1770; Spee. Served in Navy. Field of Concentration: Government.

Bobby Kennedy then attended St. Paul's School in New Hampshire, Portsmouth Priory in Rhode Island, and finished high school at Milton Academy in Massachusetts. At Milton he played on the tennis team—he still plays often, and his game, above average but not exceptional, depends more upon energy than finesse—and he quarterbacked the football team. Although he weighed barely 150 pounds, he obviously relished physical contact, and when he tackled opponents, a faculty member recalls, "they would crumble like a cathedral." Bobby showed exceptional courage, too, in joining the glee club; he and a tune have never been able to find each other.

Perhaps to save his voice, he neither smoked nor drank, twin abstinences that won him from his father, when he reached twenty-one, a bonus of $2,000. By the time he left Milton, the United States, despite his father's efforts, was at war. Encouraged by his brother Joe, by then a naval aviator, Bobby joined the V-5 naval-aviation program and went off to Bates College in Maine for eight months. Then he transferred into V-12, for officers' training, and shifted to Harvard.

All the pictures on this page were taken at Harvard. Photograph at top left was taken by the Athletic Association of all the members of the football team. The picture and descriptive material next to it appeared in the 1948 Yearbook. Below, Kennedy and three other members of the football team on the steps of the Varsity Club.

These pictures were recently discovered in a Kennedy family scrapbook. In top photo, John Kennedy is facing camera while Robert Kennedy is either walking or dancing away. Other pictures illustrate early examples of the athleticism and competitiveness for which Bob Kennedy has become famous.

In July, 1944, Joe Kennedy Jr. volunteered to pilot a plane filled with explosives across the English Channel, aim it at German submarine pens on the Belgian coast, and parachute out of his plane. Just before he was to parachute out, the plane exploded, and Joe Kennedy was killed; posthumously, he was awarded the Navy Cross. Jack Kennedy had earlier won the Navy and Marine Corps Medal for his heroism in helping save his crew after a Japanese destroyer sliced his boat, PT-109, in half. The death of Joe Jr. stunned Bobby as it did the rest of the family; it gave birth to a fatalistic attitude, which grew more pronounced after the assassination of John Kennedy. At nineteen, Bobby quit Harvard, enlisted in the Navy, and, through a family friend, Secretary of the Navy James Forrestal, got assigned to a new destroyer, the *U.S.S. Joseph P. Kennedy Jr.* Frustratingly, with his urge for combat, Bobby saw no action. He spent most of his tour cruising in the Caribbean.

Released by the Navy in 1946, Bobby, who had as a child met Churchill and corresponded with Roosevelt, discovered precinct politics. His brother Jack

sought the Democratic nomination for Congress from Boston's Eleventh District, and, to help, Bobby walked door-to-door through industrial East Cambridge — a Rolls-Royce would have been bad for the image — and asked people to vote for Kennedy. Jack won the primary, a guarantee of election, and Bobby, after a brief visit to South America, reentered Harvard. The war had not noticeably sharpened his scholastic instincts. "I didn't go to class very much, to tell you the truth," he said. "I used to talk and argue a lot, mostly about sports and politics."

He turned most of his energies to football. He was still too small for the game, but he refused to admit it. He wanted to play end. "He played on guts," said teammate David Mazzone. "He had no right to be on the varsity team," said Kenny O'Donnell, eventually captain of the team and later an aide to both Bobby and Jack Kennedy. But Bobby pushed himself and punished himself, once collapsing in a practice session with a broken leg. Tirelessly, after practice and then during the summer, he begged O'Donnell to throw him passes. "He wasn't fast, he wasn't shifty," O'Donnell said. "We had eight ends who were bigger, faster." Yet Bobby won a place on the squad, and, finally, in his senior year, despite a leg that was braced and taped, he got into the end of the Yale game, helped make a tackle, and, for playing against Yale, earned his Harvard "H," an honor that had eluded both his older and bigger brothers.

Bobby majored in government at Harvard, without distinction, and attended as

At the University of Virginia Law School, Bob Kennedy became president of the student forum, bringing to campus as speakers Justice William O. Douglas, Senator Joseph McCarthy, Ralph Bunche, his father, and his brother Jack, who was by then in the House of Representatives.

93

few parties as possible. "Nobody who goes to those things all the time makes any real contribution," he said later. After graduation in 1948, he journeyed to the Middle East and, as a foreign correspondent for *The Boston Post*, covered the Arab-Israeli war. He admired the Israelis' "spirit and zest and determination and discipline."

His newspaper stories were not distinguished; no one demanded that he make a career of journalism—or any other special field. "I had led a pretty relaxed life," Bobby conceded. "I thought I was completely unprepared and ill-equipped, so I decided to go to law school." His Harvard marks did not lead him to the more prestigious law schools. He enrolled at the University of Virginia Law School (where he once lived for ten days in his car when housing was scarce) and devoted himself more to the student forum than to his studies.

Bobby became president of the forum, and attracted to the Virginia campus several impressive speakers, ranging, ideologically, from Supreme Court Justice William O. Douglas to Republican Senator Joseph McCarthy. Despite heated resistance from campus segregationists, stirring up a fight that drew national attention, Bobby brought Ralph Bunche to the forum. He also brought in his father, and Joseph Kennedy responded to his son's introduction with a rousing isolationist speech, advocating American withdrawal from Korea and from Europe, a stand that prompted *Pravda* to publish the speech in its entirety.

During his last two years at Harvard and his first two years at Virginia, Bobby dated Ethel Skakel, the sixth of seven children of George Skakel, a millionaire and a Roman Catholic. Bobby had met Ethel for the first time in 1944, at a Canadian ski lodge, but for two years, he had dated her older sister Pat. Ethel quickly became a Kennedy buff; she roomed with Bobby's younger sister Jean at Manhattanville College of the Sacred Heart, campaigned for Jack Kennedy in 1946, and wrote her college thesis on Jack Kennedy's book *Why England Slept*. She got an A, and eventually she got Bobby, too. She seemed perfectly suited to Bobby, as spirited as he, as competitive, as interested in sports. They were married June 17, 1950, in her home town, Greenwich, Connecticut, and John Kennedy was best man.

Bobby and Ethel Kennedy got through his whole senior year at the University of Virginia Law School—and one month afterward—before they produced their first child. Bobby, still not the scholar, graduated fifty-sixth in a class of 125; and then, in June, 1951, armed like 124 others with his Virginia Law degree, he set out to find a career. He had nothing going for him except his own drive and his own ability, and his father's millions and his brother's blossoming political career.

They looked very young because they were.

R. F. K.

(below) Bobby and Ethel are joined by Eunice Kennedy, who is a bridesmaid. John Kennedy is the best man. Thus on June 17, 1950, in Greenwich, Connecticut, the population explosion was triggered.

June 12, 1954. The Army-McCarthy Hearings. Sitting directly beneath the television camera is Robert Kennedy, then counsel to the Democratic minority members of the McCarthy Subcommittee on Investigations. Sitting opposite are Senator McCarthy and subcommittee chief counsel, Roy Cohn. The day before Kennedy and Cohn almost came to blows.

CHAPTER FIVE

THE
SENATOR
AND
THE
TEAMSTER

Born in the bloodshed of Korea and buried in the emerging conflict of Vietnam, the 1950s were marked by the only Republican Administration most living Americans have known, by the insistent presence of the Cold War, and by the professional excellence of the New York Yankees. Men born in the nineteenth century—Khrushchev, Churchill, Eisenhower, Adenauer, de Gaulle, Pope John, and Casey Stengel—endured to dominate the middle of the twentieth. Robert Francis Kennedy spent most of the decade immersed in the law. But the young lawyer never argued a case in the courtroom.

His experiences varied, of course. From law school, he joined the Justice Department, working at $4,200 a year in the Criminal Division, helping to unearth corruption in the Truman Administration; in 1952 he managed his brother's successful bid for the Senate, and in 1956 his unsuccessful bid for the Vice Presidency; in 1953 he served briefly, and restlessly, as counsel to the Hoover Commission examining government operations; and in 1955 he toured Central Asia with Justice William Douglas. Once, at a banquet, their hosts offered Kennedy and Douglas a special delicacy—the eyes plucked from a goat. "For the sake of America, Bob," counseled Justice Douglas, "make like it's an oyster."

But in the 1950s, above all else, in effort and significance, Bobby Kennedy was an investigator.

He worked for the United States Senate, and his career as an investigator spread over three distinct periods: first as an assistant counsel to the entire Permanent Subcommittee on Investigations; then as chief counsel to the minority members of the subcommittee; finally, after the Democrats captured the Senate, as chief counsel to the full subcommittee and to its controversial offspring, the Senate Select Committee on Improper Activities in the Labor and Management Field.

Two men pervaded his life as an investigator, and their impact was so great

R. F. K.

In foreground, Senators John McClellan and Stuart Symington. In background, Roy Cohn and Senator Carl Mundt about to walk past Kennedy.

that even now, with one of them dead and the other in prison, they exert an influence upon his image and his ambitions. One was Senator Joseph R. McCarthy of Wisconsin, the other James Riddle Hoffa of Detroit, and they shared, besides a gruff personableness and a hunger for power, a glaring disregard for principle.

McCarthy came first. He was, in the early 1950s, at the peak of his demagogic power. Chairman of the Subcommittee on Investigations, he had accused the State Department of harboring countless communists and homosexuals, had crushed people's reputations and destroyed their jobs, and, worst, had built an

By January 21, 1955, when this picture was taken, McCarthy had been censured, Senator John McClellan had become chairman of the Subcommittee, and Robert Kennedy the Subcommittee chief counsel.

atmosphere of suspicion in the United States. This man who used his power so indiscriminately, if not ruthlessly, was a good friend of the Kennedy family. He had played touch football and softball with Bobby and Jack at Hyannis Port, had dated their sister Pat in Washington, and had welcomed a sizable campaign contribution, for his 1952 Senate race, from Joseph Kennedy Sr. Perhaps coincidentally, in 1952, McCarthy had not urged his enthusiastic anti-communist Roman Catholic followers in Massachusetts to vote for his fellow Republican, Senator Henry Cabot Lodge, who was defending his seat against John F. Kennedy.

At the end of 1952, after his work in the Justice Department and on his brother's campaign, Bobby Kennedy needed a job, and the Subcommittee on Investigations needed a lawyer. John Kennedy, who was just entering the Senate, argued against the position, but Joe Kennedy, who admired McCarthy's anti-communism, favored it. Bobby liked the idea, and, not hurt by his father's influence, joined the subcommittee in January, 1953, as an assistant to Francis Flanagan, the general counsel. While Bobby Kennedy has never indicated or conceded that he shared McCarthy's zeal, he did say, of the committee's anti-communism, "I felt it was work that needed to be done then."

Certainly, early in 1953, with the Korean War still raging, Kennedy did constructive work. He investigated reports that Allied countries were shipping goods to Communist China; and in May, he informed the subcommittee that 162 ships flying Allied flags had traded with Communist China already in 1953 and that two ships flying British flags had actually transported Red Chinese troops. The following month McCarthy put the entire subcommittee staff under the direction of Roy Cohn, an arrogantly brilliant young New Yorker who had served the Justice Department as a specialist on internal subversion. Until then, Cohn, as chief counsel, and Flanagan, as general counsel, had divided responsibility. Kennedy

This picture was taken on December 7, 1954, after Kennedy had broken politically with McCarthy. He never publicly renounced McCarthy, and attended his funeral in Appleton, Wisconsin.

99

In this picture made in June, 1956, McClellan and Kennedy have taken over. McCarthy was reduced to carping bitterly and ineffectively.

had only contempt for both Cohn and his friend, G. David Schine, who performed for the subcommittee as a consultant on communism. "Most of the investigations were instituted on the basis of some preconceived notion by the chief counsel or his staff members," Kennedy later wrote, "and not on the basis of any information that had been developed. Cohn and Schine claimed they knew from the outset what was wrong; and they were not going to let the facts interfere. . . . No real spadework that might have destroyed some of their pet theories was ever undertaken. I thought Senator McCarthy made a mistake in allowing the committee to operate in such a fashion, told him so, and resigned."

In recent years Kennedy has carefully pointed out that he did not work directly for McCarthy or Cohn, but for Flanagan, and that he stayed on the job only six months—all of which is true, but almost irrelevant. It was McCarthy's committee, his reputation was already established, and no man of even vaguely liberal bent would have sought a position with him. Significantly, the three Democratic members of the subcommittee—Senators McClellan, Jackson, and Symington—walked out in protest before Kennedy did.

The truth, evidently, is that Kennedy had few objections to McCarthy personally or to the aims of the subcommittee, only to its tactics. Because McCarthy tried to persuade him that the tactics would change, and because he felt, as he later wrote, "one of McCarthy's greatest mistakes was that he was loyal beyond reason to Roy Cohn and G. David Schine," Kennedy delayed his resignation until July 31, 1953.

Kennedy told McCarthy he planned to enter private practice, but, instead, he joined the Hoover Commission, whose membership included his father. Bobby Kennedy remained with the commission six months, then, bored by the drudgery, accepted an offer to serve as counsel to McClellan, Jackson, and Symington, who were rejoining the subcommittee to fight McCarthy from within. The offer from the minority supports Kennedy's contention that he quickly was disillusioned about McCarthy's conduct of the subcommittee. Kennedy may also have been lured back, partly, by the prospect of confrontations with Roy Cohn.

Beginning in February, 1954, Kennedy fed the Democratic minority ammunition to use both in questioning witnesses and in harassing McCarthy and Cohn. Sometimes Kennedy himself interrupted Cohn and embarrassed him. When the Army-McCarthy hearings opened in May, the tension between the two multiplied, and in June they came close to physical combat. Bobby Kennedy would have enjoyed it.

During a hearing on June 11, Senator Jackson wryly ridiculed a plan called "Deminform," Schine's gradiose and rather comical scheme to wage psychological warfare against communism. Cohn was furious. He approached Kennedy after the session and snapped, "Tell your friend Scoop Jackson we're going to get him on Monday."

"Get lost," Kennedy responded.

"You have a personal hatred," suggested Cohn.

"If I have," said Kennedy, "it's justified."

"Do you want to fight now?" said Cohn.

Kennedy, no bigger than Cohn, but considerably more athletic, elected not to spar in public. He walked away. "Do you think you're qualified to sit here?" Cohn shouted. "Do you think you're qualified?"

When Cohn later told reporters "Oh, we've got a cute kid here," he was not referring to Kennedy's boyish charm. Ten years later, when Kennedy was Attorney General, Cohn was indicted for perjury—and found not guilty. "Everyone who's followed history," said Cohn, "knows the Attorney General hates my guts." The appraisal sounded accurate.

May 6, 1957. McCarthy's casket is carried down the steps of the Capitol by Marine honor guard.

101

With the elections of 1954, followed by the Senate censure, McCarthy lost both his chairmanship and his power, Cohn drifted out of government work, John McClellan became chairman of the subcommittee, and Kennedy became chief counsel. McCarthy remained a member of the subcommittee, and Kennedy retained an affection for him. "He got so involved with all that publicity . . . he was on a toboggan," Kennedy once said. "It was so . . . exhilarating as he went downhill that it didn't matter to him if he hit a tree at the bottom. Cohn and Schine took him up the mountain and showed him all those wonderful things. He destroyed himself . . . for publicity. . . . I felt sorry for him, particularly . . . when he was such a beaten, destroyed person. . . .

"I liked him and yet at times he was terribly heavy-handed. . . . He wanted so desperately to be liked. He was so thoughtful and yet so unthoughtful in what he did to others. He was sensitive and yet insensitive. . . ."

Kennedy's sympathy for McCarthy lingered, and in 1955, when he was honored at a banquet as one of the Junior Chamber of Commerce's Ten Outstanding Young Men, he walked out before Edward R. Murrow, a courageous McCarthy foe, could deliver an anti-McCarthy speech. Two years later, Bobby Kennedy flew to Appleton, Wisconsin, to attend Joe McCarthy's funeral.

In 1955 and 1956, with Kennedy as chief counsel, McClellan's committee continued a few of the investigations initiated by McCarthy and Cohn, looked once more into Western trade with Red China, then turned away from its preoccupation with communism and examined conflict-of-interest charges against members of the Eisenhower Administration. Kennedy's investigation prompted three major officials, including Air Force Secretary Harold Talbott, to resign.

Then came Jimmy Hoffa.

In the summer of 1956, Clark Mollenhoff, an excellent investigative reporter based in Washington, persuaded Kennedy that the subcommittee should inspect the operations of the International Brotherhood of Teamsters. Kennedy and his investigators pursued Mollenhoff's tip, and quickly they found solid evidence of misuse of Teamster funds, enough evidence so that in January, 1957, despite the political sensitivity of the subject, the Senate established its Select Committee on Improper Activities in the Labor and Management Field, popularly called the Rackets Committee. The Rackets Committee drew four members from the McClellan committee and four from the Senate Labor Committee, including the junior senator from Massachusetts, John F. Kennedy.

Armed with a sizable staff, ample funds, and the confidence of Chairman McClellan, Bobby Kennedy began amassing evidence of corruption among the Teamsters. He received considerable help from reporters at work in the field, particularly Ed Guthman, a Pulitzer Prize winner in Seattle, Pierre Salinger, preparing an exposé for *Collier's*, and John Seigenthaler, an aggressive young Nashville newspaperman. All three later served in the Kennedy Administration; ironically, Clark Mollenhoff, who triggered the investigation that focused so much national attention upon Bobby and Jack Kennedy, later broke violently with the

Bob Kennedy took this picture of Patricia Kennedy Lawford, Jean Kennedy, and Ethel in Leningrad in 1955.

two brothers and became one of Bobby's most vocal critics ("the Kennedys don't tolerate dissent," Mollenhoff says).

The Rackets Committee's first target was Dave Beck, the president of the Teamsters, a man Bobby Kennedy despised as much for "mothering" his own son, for turning him into a "jellyfish," as he did for abusing his union office. Kennedy and his staff—accountant Carmine Bellino (whose sister-in-law, Angie Novello, became Kennedy's secretary) was a wizard at spotting incriminating figures— soon exposed Beck's juggling of union funds. By the end of 1957 the union president was heading to jail. To replace him, the Teamsters chose Jimmy Hoffa.

The classic confrontation—the Harvard millionaire against the unlettered tough from the slums, the man who couldn't be bought against the man who figured everybody had a price, Kennedy versus Hoffa—eventually obscured much of the Rackets Committee's work. The committee exposed corruption in many unions and many companies, but the spotlight shone on the fight between Hoffa and Kennedy, dramatic, bitter, and inevitably personal. Once, when Kennedy and Salinger wearily left their office for home at 1 a.m., they drove past the Teamsters' headquarters. Kennedy saw a light glowing in Hoffa's office. "If he's still at work," said Kennedy, "we ought to be." He returned to his desk for two more hours.

Hoffa spoke of Kennedy only with bitter contempt. "He's a spoiled kid," Hoffa said. "He's a parasite who has to work for the government because he wouldn't know how to make an honest living."

Kennedy, although he always insisted his feud was with corruption, not with Hoffa, returned the compliment. "Hoffa is evil," he said. "The Hoffas can destroy this country."

The first time Kennedy and Hoffa met, at the Washington home of a mutual acquaintance, before Hoffa had ever appeared in front of the Rackets Committee, the tone of their relationship was set.

1957. Robert Kennedy, chief counsel for the Senate Rackets Committee, and James R. Hoffa, President of the Teamsters Union hold one of their many friendly exchanges of views.

"I do to others what they do to me," said Hoffa, "only worse."

"Maybe I should have worn my bulletproof vest," said Kennedy.

Midway through the meeting, Ethel Kennedy phoned her husband. "Better hurry up, Bobby," said Hoffa, as Kennedy walked to the phone. "She probably called to see if you are still alive."

Kennedy lifted the receiver. "I'm still alive, dear," he said. "If you hear a big explosion, I probably won't be."

When Kennedy departed, Hoffa said, "Tell your wife I'm not as bad as everyone thinks I am." Instead, Kennedy told his wife, and his friends, that no one who talked as much as Hoffa about being tough could actually be so tough. The second time they confronted each other, Kennedy challenged Hoffa to a duel of pushups. Kennedy said he could do fifty; Hoffa said he could do twenty-seven; neither did any.

Most of the Kennedy-Hoffa meetings took place, of course, in the hearing room; they met as interrogator and witness. Almost always, Hoffa glared at Kennedy. "I called it 'the look,'" Kennedy later wrote, "... a deep, strange, penetrating expression of intense hatred ... the look of a man obsessed by his enmity ... this stare of absolute evilness."

104

Kennedy almost destroyed his opponent in the first round of their fight. A week before his initial encounter with Hoffa, a lawyer named Cye Cheasty came to Bobby with stunning information. Cheasty said Hoffa had offered him $2,000 a month if he would join the McClellan committee as an investigator and then pass committee documents to Hoffa. Kennedy listened to the story, became convinced of its accuracy, and immediately enlisted Cheasty as a double agent. Cheasty pretended to be Hoffa's spy on the committee; instead, he was the committee's spy on Hoffa. The FBI monitored meetings between Cheasty and Hoffa, and, one month after Cheasty entered Kennedy's office, arrested Hoffa "in possession [of] documents from the committee files. . . ."

Bobby Kennedy considered the case against Hoffa unbeatable. "What will you do if Hoffa is acquitted?" someone asked him.

"I'll jump off the Capitol," said Kennedy.

Hoffa was acquitted. His lawyer, Edward Bennett Williams, conducted a masterful defense; Hoffa himself testified that he had never suspected Cheasty worked for the committee, that he had simply wanted to hire him as a lawyer; and the Justice Department, Kennedy complained, prosecuted the case ineptly.

Ed Williams offered to send Kennedy a parachute.

Williams, who had once represented Joe McCarthy, was not always so generous to Kennedy, especially to Kennedy's legal talents. At one point during the final Hoffa hearings, Kennedy interrupted Williams, "I don't quite understand. . . ." Williams countered quickly: "I do not expect you to. I think the lawyers on the committee will."

Kennedy's exchanges with Hoffa were often equally painful, and considerably longer. One historic conversation dealt with Hoffa's purchase of Minifons, tiny electronic recording devices:

Hoffa: "What did I do with them? Well, what did I do with them?"

Kennedy: "What did you do with them?"

Hoffa: "I am trying to recall."

Kennedy: "You could remember that."

Hoffa: "When were they delivered, do you know? That must have been quite a while."

Kennedy: "You know what you did with the Minifons and don't ask me."

Hoffa: "What did I do with them?"

Kennedy: "What did you do with them?"

Finally, Hoffa summarized his testimony on the Minifons. "Well," he said, "I will have to stand on the answers that I have made in regards to my recollection, and I cannot answer unless you give me some recollection, other than I have answered."

Hoffa's strategy in his appearances before the committee was transparent. He would not claim the Fifth Amendment, but he would not remember anything of significance. He would claim that other people would know the answers; the other people would invariably cite the Fifth Amendment.

"I want to find out what information you have, Mr. Hoffa," said Kennedy once.

"Well," said Hoffa candidly, "I would like to find out what you got."

The elusiveness of Hoffa and his fellow Teamster officials, who sought refuge in the legitimate sanctions of the Fifth Amendment and their faulty memories, exasperated Kennedy, and drove him to questionable exchanges:

Kennedy: "Do you feel that if you gave a truthful answer to this committee on your taking of three hundred and twenty thousand dollars of union funds that that might tend to incriminate you?"

Dave Beck: "It might."

Kennedy: "Is that right?"

Beck: "It might."

Kennedy: "You feel that yourself?"

Beck: "It might."

Kennedy: "I feel the same way."

At a later hearing, facing Joey Glimco, the president of a Teamster local in Chicago, Kennedy again resorted to insinuation:

Kennedy: "And you defraud the union?"

Glimco: "I respectfully decline to answer because I honestly believe my answer might tend to incriminate me."

Kennedy: "I would agree with you. . . . You haven't got the guts to [answer], have you, Mr. Glimco?"

Kennedy's personal attacks upon witnesses, and his refusal—unavoidably reminiscent of McCarthy—to accept the Fifth Amendment as a perfectly legal response, inspired in many liberals, who had no use for Hoffa or his henchmen, a distaste and a distrust that persists. Professor Alexander Bickel of Yale Law School charged that the committee, "with Mr. Kennedy in the lead . . . embarked on a number of purely punitive expeditions [involving] relentless, vindictive battering [of witnesses]. . . . Mr. Kennedy appears to find congenial the role of prosecutor, judge, and jury, all consolidated in his one, efficient person."

Yet Joseph Rauh, former national chairman of the Americans for Democratic Action, arguing in Kennedy's behalf, was charitable to his instincts, if not to his skills. "He was trying to be a fair investigator," said Rauh, "and any abuses were not due to 'vindictiveness,' but to his lack of experience. If it sometimes led to abuse of witnesses, it sometimes led to witnesses like Hoffa getting away with murder. The technique of questioning is an art, and Bobby wasn't experienced at it—he didn't know how to go for the jugular."

Pierre Salinger, a biased observer, added another defense: "Bob Kennedy had a firm rule that he would introduce no evidence before the committee that was not provable in a court of law."

Kennedy himself remained sensitive to the charges against him. "There were from thirty to one hundred and twenty reporters there," he once said, "and if there had been any such abuses, you'd think they would have come up with one or two samples at the time." The weakness of this defense is that reportorial laziness is no more uncommon than union corruption. To take a more reasonable line of defense, Kennedy seemed firmly to believe that (1) by lusting after corrupt leaders, he was saving the little man in the union, the worker exploited by both

Ten years Later. Hoffa, raincoat covering handcuffs, enters the Federal Prison at Lewisburg, Pennsylvania.

management and labor, and (2) he was justified in insinuating misconduct once he was convinced of the existence of the misconduct. Still, accepting both points, Kennedy did appear overzealous, too willing to bypass a witness's rights simply to score a point. He was, obviously, exhilarated by the contest. "It was like playing Notre Dame every day," he said.

The pressures of the game, aside from the time- and energy-consuming demands of thorough investigation, were immense. Straight partisan political pressure was inescapable, and generally ignored; Kennedy pressed an investigation that led to the conviction of the Democratic Mayor of Gary, Indiana. But Bobby and Jack Kennedy shared a delicate position. Everyone knew their eye was on the Presidency in 1960. "You tell Bobby Kennedy for me," Hoffa once said, "that he's not going to make his brother President over Hoffa's dead body." The Kennedys welcomed the attention drawn by the Rackets Committee, but they had to avoid appearing antilabor. Both of them, whenever possible, praised instances of honest unionism; they especially lauded Walter Reuther, the president of the United Auto Workers, although Bobby did bring out cases of UAW misconduct. While Republican members of the committee wanted nothing more than to discredit the ultra-liberal Reuther, the investigative staff found no evidence of personal corruption. In 1960, Reuther was an early supporter of John Kennedy for President; Hoffa, at the head of his 1,700,000 Teamsters, was not.

At least two minor aspects of the committee's work amused Bobby Kennedy.

Once he had to question a madam—a house keeper, not a home keeper—and the experience unnerved him. "A call house," he said at a hearing, "is distinguished from a regular house of ill fame . . . sometimes known as a walk-in, by the fact that the clientele is a select one. . . . A house of ill fame, or a walk-in, will accept anyone who comes to the premises. Another, another feature, another feature of, of the call house is. . . ." He gave up to laughter.

He enjoyed, too, the investigation into the ownership of an office building on

Fourteenth Street in New York City, headquarters for several labor unions. Kennedy suspected that gangsters might own the building. He sent investigators to check the records. They reported back that the building was owned by the Kennedy family.

Kennedy quit the committee in 1959 and spent the summer at his Virginia home, writing, with the editing aid of John Seigenthaler, his personal account of the labor investigation. *The Enemy Within*, as much an assault upon Jimmy Hoffa as anything else, became a bestseller; the combination of its success and its style may have cost Bobby Kennedy the literary vote.

Kennedy's active investigative tour was ended, but his war with Jimmy Hoffa was not. Two years later, as Attorney General, he appointed a fifteen-man team to investigate labor and management racketeering. The Justice Department team was soon nicknamed the "Get-Hoffa Squad." Eventually it got Hoffa—but not without difficulty.

For several years Hoffa slipped in and out of court cases, beating back charges, flailing at Kennedy. "If this kid don't get away from this crusade," Hoffa said, "he's going to crack up. I talk to people who go to parties with him, and they say he's got one topic of conversation—Hoffa. He's got to flip."

The crusade to get Hoffa was indeed ruthless, justifiably ruthless by Kennedy's measurement. The Justice Department employed walkie-talkies, electronic recording devices, cameras, informers, pressure, harassment, every conceivable tactic to pin a criminal charge upon Hoffa. Finally, the Justice Department scored —with a spy, Edward Grady Partin, hidden among Hoffa's entourage.

Partin, an ex-convict and jailbreaker once indicted on charges of embezzling $1,600 in Teamster funds, reported to the Get-Hoffa Squad that Hoffa was attempting to bribe jurors in Chattanooga, Tennessee. On March 4, 1964, after an extended and complicated court battle, a Chattanooga jury convicted Hoffa on two counts of attempted bribery. At a victory party in Washington, the Get-Hoffa Squad gave Bobby Kennedy another present, a wallet bearing the jury foreman's statement of Hoffa's guilt.

For three years, with appeals that stretched unsuccessfully up to the Supreme Court, and with liberal groups protesting the manner in which Hoffa had been trapped, the Teamster president stayed out of jail. Finally, on Tuesday, March 7, 1967, he began serving a five-year prison sentence.

It had taken Bobby Kennedy fully a decade to put Jimmy Hoffa behind bars, and perhaps a more accomplished lawyer would have done it sooner. Bobby Kennedy, in his first ten years as a lawyer, had learned a great deal about many things, but not necessarily a great deal about the practice of law.

When he took over the Justice Department, he was negotiating a contract for the movie version of *The Enemy Within*. Joseph P. Kennedy, the old moviemaker, examined the contract and demanded a change.

"But your son, the Attorney General, said he was satisfied with the way that clause was drawn," argued a studio executive.

"What the hell," said Joe Kennedy, "does he know about it?"

Bob Kennedy was known as a voracious worker as well as eater. Here he is shown combining both activities in a picture taken in 1957 (by Paul Schutzer, who was killed in the Arab-Israeli War, June 1967).

CHAPTER SIX

ALL
THE
WAY
WITH
J.F.K.

Some people called him "Raúl," after Castro's belligerent kid brother. Some called him "the little monster." Hubert Humphrey once called him "that greedy little . . ." incomplete sentence. But nobody called him lazy, nobody called him inefficient, and nobody called him wrong. As a political campaign manager, helping to steer his brother from the House of Representatives to the White House, Robert Kennedy did not always win friends, but he did influence people. He influenced their votes.

Bobby Kennedy sampled political campaigning in 1948, the first time his brother ran for Congress, but he functioned in the background, taking orders, not giving them; after all, he cleared the voting age by only a year. But, in 1952, when Joseph Kennedy Sr. and John Kennedy agreed to bid for the Senate, they chose Bobby to manage the campaign. He was only twenty-six, only a year out of law school, and the Irish professionals who have played so major a role in Massachusetts Democratic politics did not fully appreciate his youthful enthusiasm.

Bobby antagonized almost everyone, starting at the top with Governor Paul Dever, who was running for reelection. Bobby marched up to Dever one day, informed the governor he had made a mistake that might harm J.F.K.'s campaign, and warned the governor to be more careful. Dever furiously ordered Bobby out, then phoned Joe Kennedy. "I know you're an important man around here and all that," said Dever, "but I'm telling you this and I mean it: Keep that fresh kid of yours out of my sight from now on."

Dever's sentiments won support in the political establishment. "Those politicians," said Bobby, "just wanted to sit around and talk about it and have their pictures taken at the rallies." He suggested they lick envelopes, ring doorbells, get out and work; the notion repelled them. "Every politician in Massachusetts was mad at Bobby," John Kennedy said later, "but we had the best organization in history. You can't make an omelet without breaking the egg."

November 5, 1952. John F. Kennedy won Henry Cabot Lodge's seat in the Senate by 70,000 votes of 2,300,000 cast. Although Bob Kennedy was only 26, his father and brother selected him to manage the campaign.

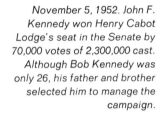

As skillful as he was at breaking eggs, Bobby was not a natural chef. "I don't think he was enamored of political organization, with all its nuts and bolts," said Larry O'Brien, a consummate politician who, with Kenny O'Donnell, helped Bobby run the campaign. "It's not glamorous. It's not the kind of work he'd pick over an extended period of years. But he applied himself vigorously." Bobby needed 2,500 signatures on a petition to secure John Kennedy the Democratic nomination; he collected 262,324. "We tried to organize every town of over six hundred voting population," Bobby said. The organization produced a network of 268 local leaders, backed by 28,000 volunteer workers. He stressed voter-registration drives; 100,000 new voters enrolled. Bobby drove himself as many as twenty hours a day, seven days a week, and he lost ten pounds. The pace of the campaign had to be brutal. John Kennedy was battling a respected incumbent, Henry Cabot Lodge, and an Eisenhower tide that would sweep every other Massachusetts Democrat out of statewide office.

Joseph Kennedy willingly invested close to $500,000 in the campaign, and, by 70,000 votes of 2,300,000 cast, John Kennedy won a seat in the United States Senate. Joe Kennedy, always a shrewd investor, looked beyond the Senate, to the White House.

His vision seemed audacious, yet in 1956, only four years after he entered the Senate, John Kennedy was a candidate for the Democratic Vice-Presidential nomination. Before the convention in Chicago, Adlai Stevenson's forces assured Kennedy he was being considered as a running mate. To an impartial viewer, he appeared, at best, a remote third choice, behind Senators Estes Kefauver and Hubert Humphrey. Bobby Kennedy showed up to help improve the odds.

When John Kennedy delivered the speech nominating Adlai Stevenson for President, and when Stevenson elected to put the choice of a Vice-Presidential candi-

date before the convention, Bobby Kennedy, his family, and his friends suddenly found themselves in a frantic search for votes, a search that brought John Kennedy 304 votes on the first ballot. Nomination required 686½ votes; Kefauver had 483½; no one else was close. On the second ballot, votes began shifting, and swiftly John Kennedy moved into the lead, his total rapidly rising over 600, to the point where one or two key blocs could have given him the nomination. And then, as Bobby roamed the floor of the convention, scrambling, pleading for the decisive votes, Kefauver's candidacy abruptly caught fire and carried him to the nomination. The Kennedys hated to lose, and they spoke of doublecrosses, but Bobby soon regained his composure. He looked at his brother, and, perhaps not

(above) The John Kennedy-Jacqueline Bouvier wedding party picture taken by Bradford Bachrach in September, 1953, at Newport, Rhode Island. Robert and Ethel Kennedy stand at far right. (below) "Go out for a long one." John Kennedy pitching, Robert Kennedy catching at Hickory Hill.

1956
DEMOCRATIC
NATIONAL
CONVENTION

(left) John Kennedy made the nominating speech for Adlai Stevenson for President at the 1956 Democratic National Convention and was almost nominated himself as the Vice-Presidential candidate. Bobby told him he was lucky to lose. Bobby was right. (right) The first primary of the 1960 campaign was held in Wisconsin, where John Kennedy (with Ted Sorenson) met the folks outside a factory.

really believing his own words, he said, "This is the luckiest thing that ever happened to you."

Bobby was right. The loss of the nomination spared Kennedy the disaster of sharing defeat in 1956, and it freed Bobby, on leave from the McClellan committee, to spend seven weeks traveling with Stevenson. He traveled quietly, but he watched everything. He saw Stevenson's weaknesses, his failure to reach the crowds, his staff's failure to utilize the press properly. He studied the anatomy of a defeat, and he took careful notes. Bobby, although he was nominally the campaign manager, missed much of his brother's Senate race in 1958, when John Kennedy achieved the most decisive margin of victory in Massachusetts history, but his notes were ready when he needed them.

On October 28, 1959, sixteen people gathered in the living room of Bobby Kennedy's home in Hyannis Port. Bobby was there, and, among the others, Larry O'Brien, Kenny O'Donnell, Pierre Salinger, Ted Sorensen, Steve Smith, and John Kennedy. They met to make John Kennedy President. In the morning, J.F.K. himself led the discussion, but in the afternoon, Bobby took command. He carved out the assignments for himself and the others, and from then on he ran the campaign that would lift his brother to the Presidency. The immediate goal was the Democratic nomination, and to win that, John Kennedy had to prove himself in the primaries. He chose several mild arenas and two key battlegrounds—West Virginia and, against Bobby's advice, Wisconsin.

Wisconsin was first, and although Kennedy's main rival, Hubert Humphrey, came from the Midwest, Bobby and his troops organized such an efficient operation—Humphrey's error, said Bobby later, was that "he didn't find out until it was too late that you couldn't depend on the Wisconsin organization"—that they seemed likely to carry all ten Wisconsin districts. But Humphrey, rallying late in the campaign, captured four of the districts and 44 percent of the vote. "It wasn't as glorious an occasion as it might have been," said Bobby.

Next came West Virginia, a decisive test of the religion issue, a state with an estimated Catholic population of only 4 percent. The race was close—at one point Bobby urged Humphrey to withdraw—and bitter. Humphrey, Bobby charged, "has played fast and loose with smears and innuendoes. . . . I do not intend to take this kind of abuse indefinitely."

"Politics is a serious business," Humphrey countered, "not a boy's game where you can pick up your ball and run home if things don't go according to your idea of who should win."

The bitterness passed. On election eve Humphrey encountered Ethel Kennedy at a West Virginia airport. "When this is all over," he said, "and our temperatures are down some, I hope we can get together with our families."

The following night, after the returns had confirmed a stunningly strong Kennedy victory, Bobby Kennedy walked through a drizzle to Humphrey's headquarters, kissed a reluctant Muriel Humphrey, the senator's wife, then shook hands with the loser. Together, they walked back to Kennedy's headquarters, where Humphrey announced he was stepping out of the Presidential race.

Bobby's impish humor returned. "I couldn't have done it," he said, "without my brother."

In the two months between the West Virginia primary and the Democratic convention in Los Angeles, Bobby Kennedy's confidence grew. The nomination, he felt, was his brother's, but he wanted to make it certain, and he wanted it on the first ballot. In the thirty-six hours before the balloting for the Presidential nomination, Bobby kept up an incredible pace, plotting victory in the convention, and victory beyond. "We're not out here to go to Disneyland," he told his staff. "We're not out here to go to nightclubs. We're out here to work. If you're not, you can turn in your staff badges right now."

The day before the balloting, Bobby called a meeting in Los Angeles to organize a special campaign among Spanish-speaking Americans. "They said I was crazy," he said later, "but they made the difference in California, and they helped like hell in Texas."

The morning of the balloting, Bobby told his staff, "I want to say a few words

Jacqueline joined her husband for part of the Wisconsin (shown here) and West Virginia primaries, and proved an enormous asset.

In West Virginia, where the Catholic issue was decisive, John Kennedy is shown here talking to a farmer. " 'I couldn't have done it,' Bobby said, 'without my brother.' "

about civil rights. We have the best civil-rights plank the Democratic Party has ever had. I want you fellows to make it clear to your delegations that the Kennedy forces are unequivocally in favor of this plank. . . . Those of you who are dealing with Southern delegations make it absolutely clear how we stand. . . . Don't fuzz it up. . . . Don't let there be any doubt anywhere as to how the Kennedy people stand on this."

Kennedy dispatched aides to doublecheck each delegation, and at least one of the aides, Arthur Schlesinger, assigned to Minnesota, discovered that Bobby had, as expected, earned some enemies. "I found them resentful over the intense pressure of the Kennedy people," Schlesinger wrote, "and particularly mistrustful of Bobby Kennedy."

Finally, Bobby polled his staff to see exactly how the voting shaped up. "I don't want generalities or guesses," he said. "There's no point in fooling ourselves. I want the cold facts. I want to hear only the votes we are guaranteed on the first ballot." The total came to 740, twenty-one short of victory. "We can't miss a trick in the next twelve hours," said Bobby. "If we don't win tonight, we're dead."

A late surge of Stevenson enthusiasm threatened to deadlock the convention, perhaps even to throw the nomination to Lyndon Johnson. Bobby worried about the Stevenson strength, but he predicted victory on the first ballot.

During the balloting, Bobby directed operations from a command post in a model home outside the Los Angeles Sports Arena. By phone, he ordered one staff member to try to persuade the governor of New Jersey to give his votes to Kennedy. "Go tell Bob Meyner," said Bobby, "that we're going to win this thing

116

(left to right) On the convention floor. Bob Kennedy exchanges ritualistic political grips with Carmine DeSapio (while Robert Wagner watches) and Stewart Udall,

on the first ballot, and this is his last chance. He either switches his delegation to us or he's going to be rolled over."

"Meyner's going to stand pat on the first ballot," the staffer reported. "He doesn't think we can make it the first time around and will take the votes himself as a favorite son."

Without New Jersey, John Kennedy's vote total rose, and as the balloting progressed alphabetically, Bobby realized that Wyoming's fifteen votes could end the contest. He telephoned his brother Teddy, stationed with the Wyoming delegation. "Tell them if we have all fifteen," Bobby said, "Wyoming will cinch the nomination of the next President."

Teddy relayed the message, and, almost on cue, the Wyoming chairman rose and announced, "Wyoming casts all fifteen votes for the next President of the United States."

Watching on television, Bobby Kennedy leaped to his feet with a shout. Now his brother was bidding to become the youngest man and the first Catholic to be elected President of the United States. Additionally, as Bobby said, "he was running at a time when there was no great upheaval, when times were relatively prosperous, against a man who had visited fifty-five countries and talked to kings and queens and emperors, who was the legal heir to the most popular man in American history."

Bobby's battle against Richard Nixon began early the following morning. At 9 a.m. he met all fifty state chairmen and stressed one of his favorite themes, the importance of a voter-registration drive. The same morning, Schlesinger wanted to talk to Bobby about repairing relations with the Stevenson forces. "Arthur," said Bobby, "human nature requires that you allow us forty-eight hours. Adlai has given us a rough time over the last three days. In forty-eight hours, I will do anything you want, but right now I don't want to hear anything about the Stevensonians."

Bob Kennedy, Ted Sorensen, and Pierre Salinger in a hotel suite.

*and listens to rare wisdom from Mayor Daley of Chicago. (far right) Sargent Shriver
and Kenny O'Donnell snag delegates on the convention floor.*

Most of the day focused upon the selection of John Kennedy's running mate. Reports vary of the debate that led, finally, to Lyndon Johnson's nomination, but Bobby's role seems fairly clear. He opposed Johnson at the start, but once his brother decided to offer Johnson the nomination, Bobby acquiesced. Apparently, neither Bobby nor his brother thought, at first, that Johnson would accept. When Johnson's willingness to run became clear, and a revolt began brewing among convention liberals, Bobby's task was to sound Johnson out, to see if he would fight, if necessary, for the nomination, and, if not, to give him a chance to withdraw. The suspicion that Bobby, without his brother's sanction, sought to persuade Johnson to pull out is illogical; Bobby realized that he was the campaign manager, not the candidate.

"There was no disagreement between my brother and me on this," Bobby once said. "We did, however, have our supporters to consider. Our primary aim at the convention had been to put over John Kennedy on the first ballot. We had had little time to think about the Vice-Presidential slot. We'd finally narrowed the field down to Scoop Jackson, Orville Freeman, and Lyndon. When Johnson's name was selected, I pointed out to my brother that this was going to be very hard to explain to many of our supporters. Johnson had tried to block us, to fight us all the way, and the fight had unfortunately gotten personal in the final stages.

"I was afraid the news of Johnson's selection . . . would cause the Walter Reuthers, John Baileys, and others to collapse. And some of them did fall on the floor when they got the word. We were afraid there would be a floor fight to prevent Johnson's nomination. We didn't know whether he'd be willing to go through . . . all the acrimony again. I was sent as emissary to ask him. . . . He said he was willing to risk a floor fight. . . . I went back to my brother with the news."

Bobby brought to the Presidential campaign the same urgency he had brought to the fight for the nomination. His office at Democratic headquarters bore a small sign on the door—"Dave Beck, General President"—but Bobby misused nothing

*" 'Don't let there be any doubt as to how
the Kennedy people stand on this.' "*

but other people's egos. To the Reform Democrats of New York, at war with the Regular Democrats, Bobby snapped, "Gentlemen, I don't give a damn if the state and county organizations survive after November, and I don't give a damn if you survive. I want to elect John F. Kennedy." He told Frank Sinatra and Walter Reuther that they were too controversial to campaign for his brother, and he set out to register 10,000,000 new voters. "If I were running the party," he told his brother, "I sometimes think I'd scrap everything, close up national headquarters, and spend every nickel we had on registration." He carefully orchestrated his brother's television appearances—"Bread-and-butter, peace, get Jackie . . . that religious thing, say it again"—and, in the control room before the first decisive TV debate, he studied Nixon's appearance, his pallor, sunken cheeks and eyes, his outsize collar, and he could hardly contain his pleasure. Yet, when one of Nixon's aides asked his impression of the makeup job, Bobby coolly replied, "Terrific. Terrific. I wouldn't change a thing."

Inevitably, in his harsh search for votes, Bobby made enemies. Often, when he sent his men to coordinate local groups, friction arose. "It's like the Gaza Strip," he said. "You have to watch it all the time and make sure the little fights don't become wars."

The candidate appreciated his efforts. "I don't even have to think about organization," said John Kennedy. "I just show up. He's the hardest worker. He's the greatest organizer. He's taken no time off. He's fantastic. He's living on nerves."

Joe Kennedy agreed. "Jack works harder than any mortal man," he said, with paternal overstatement. "Bobby goes a little further."

"I'm not running a popularity contest," said Bobby. "It doesn't matter if people like me or not. Jack can be nice to them. I don't try to antagonize people, but

" 'We're not out here to go to Disneyland,' Bobby told his staff. 'We're not out here to go to night clubs. We're out here to work. If you're not, you can turn in your staff badges right now.' "

(above) Larry O'Brien, Steve Smith, Bob Kennedy, and Pierre Salinger meet in Los Angeles shortly after the nomination to discuss early campaign strategy. (below) Kennedy brothers shortly after Jack's nomination at Hyannis Port.

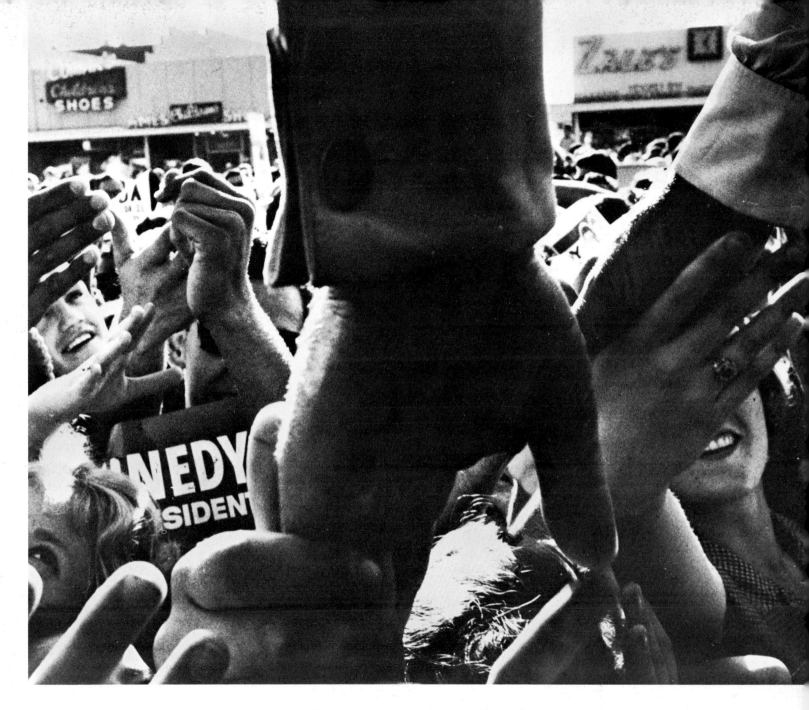

somebody has to be able to say no. If people are not getting off their behinds, how do you say that nicely?''

The Kennedys set up headquarters on election night exactly where their drive had started, in Bobby's Hyannis Port home. The returns filtered in, disappointing at first, then pointing toward a Kennedy landslide. As the landslide failed to materialize, as the margin grew thinner and thinner, Bobby Kennedy manned the telephone and analyzed the trends. Of all those who had gathered in Hyannis Port, including the candidate, only one stayed up all night to discover, in the dawn, that John Kennedy was President. The one who waited, fittingly, was Bobby Kennedy.

And then, after Nixon's concession and his brother's victory speech, Bobby unwound by playing touch football with family and friends. He played quarterback, of course, and when the President-elect of the United States dropped a pass, Bobby announced, ''That's my brother—all guts, no brains.''

John F. Kennedy had won a new job, and Bobby Kennedy had added a new layer to his image. Now, to accompany the picture of the young investigator, the sym-

It was during the campaign that John Kennedy's extraordinary physical appeal — for men as well as women — began to dominate the country.

Although the expressions on their faces make it seem unlikely, this is a picture of Kennedy and Johnson campaigning in Texas in the fall of 1960.

123

pathetic friend of Joe McCarthy and the merciless enemy of Jimmy Hoffa, Bobby Kennedy was the campaign manager, capable but demanding, effective but antagonizing. His future in politics certainly did not seem to be as a candidate, as a man dependent upon popularity.

Bobby looked ahead to the Kennedy Administration with pride. "We're going to do what we thought Eisenhower was going to do in 1952, and never did," he said. "Bring a new spirit to government, new men who believe in a cause, who believe their jobs go on forever, not just from nine to five, who believe in the United States, not just in an Administration. Our campaign was made up of new faces to a large extent, and this Administration will be made up of new faces to a large extent."

He wondered what his own role would be. "I'd like to work for the government," Bobby said, "but there are obvious difficulties now because of the relationship

thing. I wouldn't take an appointment to Jack's Senate seat. I wouldn't want any kind of a Sherman Adams job in the White House. I'd want my own position with my own authority, but there you run into the relationship problem again. I really haven't worked out the problems in my own mind."

Joe Kennedy had his solution. He wanted John Kennedy to name Bobby the Attorney General of the United States. He insisted that J.F.K. would need someone near him he could trust absolutely, that he would need Bobby. John Kennedy, logically fearing charges of nepotism, resisted. But Joe Kennedy persisted until he convinced his older son, and then Bobby resisted. He thought he might prefer a sub-Cabinet post in the State Department or the Defense Department. "I've been chasing bad guys all my life," he said. "I'd like a change."

John Kennedy began to press his brother, and Bobby wavered. He talked to J. Edgar Hoover, to Justice Douglas, to William Rogers, the retiring Attorney General. He wanted to know how the Justice Department operated, what were its strengths and weaknesses. He vacillated between acceptance and rejection of the job.

Finally, one morning in mid-December, over breakfast at his brother's house in

Georgetown, Bobby Kennedy surrendered. He would take the job; he would become, at thirty-five, the second-youngest Attorney General in the history of the United States, the youngest in 143 years, and, of course, the first brother of a President to hold the position.

"I'd like to open the door at about three a.m.," John Kennedy told a friend, "and announce that Bobby is Attorney General and then shut the door and run like hell."

When J.F.K. did announce Bobby's appointment, the predictable cries of nepotism and inexperience echoed. "If Robert Kennedy were one of the outstanding lawyers of the country," *The New York Times* editorialized, "a preeminent legal philosopher, a noted prosecutor or legal officer at Federal or State level, the situa-

The Hyannis Armory, the day after the election. Bob Kennedy and Joseph P. Kennedy, Sr., listen to John Kennedy read congratulatory telegrams from Eisenhower and Nixon (photographer crouching before them is Paul Schutzer).

126

Bob, Ethel, and Ted Kennedy play touch football on an Acapulco beach shortly after the election. The President-Elect had offered Bob the Attorney-Generalship, and he had already refused.

tion would be different. But his experience . . . is surely insufficient to warrant his present appointment.''

The President-elect deflected the criticism with humor. ''I can't see that it's wrong,'' he said, ''to give Bobby a little legal experience before he goes out to practice law.''

John Kennedy needled his brother, but he did not underestimate his value. At Christmas, 1960, the new President and his wife presented Bobby with a copy of his own book, *The Enemy Within*, bound in red leather.

''To Bobby—the brother within,'' wrote John F. Kennedy.

And Jacqueline Kennedy added her words: ''To Bobby—who made the impossible possible and changed all our lives.''

CHAPTER SEVEN

THE ASSISTANT PRESIDENT

Have you ever tried a case?

The lawyer shook his head. "I have not," Robert Kennedy told the Senate Judiciary Committee studying his appointment. "My experience is working for government. . . . I am young, and I cannot make up for the fact that I have had only ten years' experience since college."

One notable Republican member of the Judiciary Committee did not object to the new Attorney General. He praised Bobby Kennedy's work in prosecuting crime, praised his family, praised his energy. And to top his praise, Kenneth Keating argued, "His close relation to the President is an extraneous issue."

The Senate confirmed the appointment, formalizing the most extraordinary relationship that had ever existed between a President of the United States and a member of his Cabinet. In public, they called each other "Mr. President" and "the Attorney General." In private, they called each other "Jack" and "Bobby." They called each other often.

Built on mutual trust and respect, the relationship lay open to kidding and to envy. A comedian named Vaughan Meader earned fame mimicking the President; one of his routines caught J.F.K. scolding his daughter Caroline, "I want you young-sters to—ah—stop fighting—ah—amongst yourselves. Go ahead, Bobby, I think you were first." One friend of the President argued that Bobby's influence was minimal. "After a while," the friend insisted, "Jack'll say, 'Oh, shut up, Bobby.'" But the comics and the cynics could not obscure the fact that Robert Kennedy, in his middle thirties, was actually assistant President, confidant and adviser; that, in foreign affairs and broad domestic policy, he ranged far beyond the usual role of his office.

Yet his responsibilities as Attorney General came first, and although his record was not above criticism, Bobby did, almost everyone ultimately agreed, a superb job. He assembled an excellent staff. First he chose Byron "Whizzer" White, the

129

They met at the White House two or three times a week. "In public, they
called each other 'Mr. President' and 'the Attorney General.'

All-American football player and Rhodes Scholar, to be his Deputy Attorney General. Then, with White directing the talent hunt, he found men of intelligence and skill to head the divisions of the Justice Department—Archibald Cox, Burke Marshall, Louis Oberdorfer, and the two men who followed Bobby as Attorney General, Nicholas Katzenbach and Ramsey Clark. Even Professor Alexander Bickel of Yale, who had condemned Kennedy's work with the McClellan committee, and had judged him "unfit" to be Attorney General, pronounced the staff "brilliant."

Kennedy blended informality and hard work. Each morning he would enter his vast office—large enough for him and Whizzer White to pass a football back and forth—settle behind his 300-pound desk, loosen his tie, unbutton his collar, and roll up the sleeves of his tapered custom shirt. Sometimes he would put his feet up on the desk; sometimes he would pull out the bottom two drawers to use as a footrest.

He decorated his office in Kennedy modern—a bust of Lincoln, watercolors by his children, originals by William Walton, and, until he lost the heavyweight championship, an autographed picture of Floyd Patterson. Almost always, Bobby kept his door open. When he wanted an aide, he shouted. When an aide wanted him, he could enter without knocking. His powers of concentration, his ability to absorb complex material, impressed his staff.

Kennedy lifted morale in the Justice Department. Accompanied by his Newfoundland, Brumus, who could not read the rules barring dogs from government buildings, Bobby often wandered through the corridors, meeting people, asking questions, introducing himself. By the dozens, he invited members of the department's 33,000-man staff to his office. Hundreds of Justice Department employees who had never before met an Attorney General shook Bobby Kennedy's hand and chatted with him. He urged lawyers on the lower levels not to be discouraged. "After all," he said, "I came to this department ten years ago as an assistant attorney making $4,200 a year. But I had ability and integrity, an interest in my work. I stayed late hours, my brother became President, and now I'm Attorney General." Pause. "Those qualifications were not necessarily listed in their order of importance."

His aides appreciated his sense of humor—after hearing both sides of a complicated legal problem, he might say, "Well, I guess there just isn't any way of deciding this"—and they appreciated his contacts. If his staff had a problem relating to the State Department Bobby could call the Secretary of State—and get him. No previous Attorney General had such persuasive power. "There is tremendous advantage," Bobby admitted, "in having the same last name as the President of the United States."

His tolerance for laziness had not noticeably increased. During one crisis in the Justice Department, three of his aides were in his office making phone calls and a fourth was listening. Bobby picked up a copy of *The Enemy Within*, hurled it at the fourth man, and, from half a room away, hit him in the stomach. "Get to work and start doing something useful," he said.

In private, they called each other 'Jack' and 'Bobby.'

Another time, cruising the department with John Seigenthaler, Kennedy spotted an employee with his feet on his desk and a paperback in his hands. "I can't believe it," Bobby said. He turned to the avid reader. "What division are you in?" he demanded. "What are you working on?" Steel came into his voice. "Don't you realize you're employed by the Department of Justice and by the taxpayers to do a job? Read that book at home!"

The man's work improved substantially in the next few weeks, and one day Seigenthaler met him in the hall. "I wish the Attorney General would come back," the man said. "That was the first time I'd ever done that. I had nothing else to do."

Later, on a tour of Justice Department outposts, Kennedy saw a secretary reading a novel. "What's the story on that secretary?" he asked the local United States marshal.

"We've had a lot of trouble with her," said the marshal, "but she's a vet and civil service. I've complained about her, but haven't gotten anywhere. Once she called me stupid." The marshal fumbled for words. "You have to have permission from Washington to fire anyone," he said, "and they. . . ."

"You've got it," said Kennedy. As his party swept out of the marshal's office, he added, "I hope she finishes her novel."

Bobby showed no special legal talent in his job — finally, after two years in office, he argued his first case; from force of habit, he started at the top, before the Supreme Court — but his administrative gifts spurred the department to new peaks of productivity, in antitrust suits, in tax cases, in racketeering prosecutions, in almost every phase of its work. He waged war on organized crime and gambling, offered programs to combat juvenile delinquency, proposed a domestic Peace Corps, hammered out a more equitable immigration bill, and even testified against two Democratic Congressmen he was prosecuting for corruption. Arthur Schlesinger called him "the best Attorney General this country has had for a generation," and others, less committed to the Kennedy camp, agreed. With his enthusiastic pursuit of civil rights and civil liberties, he converted to his side many who, judging him by his past, had considered him illiberal.

Before he became Attorney General, Robert Kennedy's involvement and concern with civil rights was minimal. None of his best friends was Negro. Certainly he had an awareness of the problem, but it was more political than moral. More than he understood poverty and prejudice, he understood the Negro vote, and when the Reverend Martin Luther King was arrested in Georgia during John Kennedy's Presidential campaign, Bobby put in a phone call to urge Dr. King's release on bail. He won votes with his call, but he learned little about Negro problems.

Even after he had been in office for a while, he did not fully understand. He held a meeting once with James Baldwin, the author, and several of Baldwin's friends, mostly militant Negroes. The meeting suffered from a terrible communications gap. "He was surprised to hear there were Negroes who wouldn't fight for their country," said Baldwin. "How many Negroes would fight to free Cuba when they can't be free themselves? He just didn't get the point. He was naive. He doesn't know pain. He just doesn't know."

"He decorated the office in Kennedy modern — a bust of Lincoln, watercolors by his children . . ."

R.F.K. and Ed Guthman. " 'I always knew there was something about you I hated.' "

The Attorney General with two of his closest associates at the Justice Department. Above with Nicholas Katzenbach, who succeeded him. Below with Byron White, who became an Associate Justice of the Supreme Court.

If Baldwin felt bitterly disappointed in Kennedy, other Negroes active in the civil-rights movement grew to respect him. They argued with him on issues and timing, but they accepted his sincerity. His first personal step in civil rights was simply a gesture. He told the Metropolitan Club, an exclusive Washington society, that if it did not lift its ban on Negroes, he would resign. After several months, he fulfilled his threat.

While his men worked through the courts to speed desegregation in the schools, Bobby's next step was also a gesture, but a significant one. In May, 1961, he visited the University of Georgia as its Law Day speaker, and, before Southerners in a newly integrated Southern setting, he spoke on civil rights. "I happen to believe that the 1954 decision [on school segregation] was right," he said, "but my belief does not matter—it is the law. Some of you may believe the decision was wrong. That does not matter. It is the law. . . ."

Two weeks later, in Montgomery, Alabama, a mob of some 3,000 whites, untroubled by the law or by local police, assaulted a group of Freedom Riders.

"His responsibilities as Attorney General came first, and although his record was not above criticism, Bobby did, almost everyone ultimately agreed, a superb job. He assembled an excellent staff." To the left the Attorney General with part of his excellent staff — and Brumus, "who could not read the rules barring dogs from government buildings."

Negroes were brutally beaten; so was John Seigenthaler from the Justice Department. In constant touch with Kennedy by telephone, the Deputy Attorney General, Byron White, led a hastily recruited force of 400 federal officers and restored order. The next night, when Dr. King held a prayer meeting for 1,200 people, 150 federal marshals, under White's supervision, protected the meeting. Bobby could have sent in massive federal forces, but he had used restraint; now he urged restraint upon potential Freedom Riders, asking them to stay out of Alabama and Mississippi "until the present state of confusion and danger has passed." Dr. King felt Bobby was asking too much—"It's a matter of conscience and morality," the minister said—and giving too little. Yet within a week, the Justice Department filed a petition for an order to abolish segregation in airports and bus and train terminals in interstate traffic.

In a Voice of America broadcast, Kennedy condemned the violence of Montgomery, but spoke hopefully of progress. "There's no question," he said, "that in the next thirty or forty years a Negro can also achieve the same position that my brother has as President of the United States."

He campaigned in the courts and in Congress to bring the Negro better education and more voting rights. At one Senate hearing, when Kennedy ridiculed the transparent devices used in the South to prevent educated Negroes from voting, Senator Sam Ervin of North Carolina defended the literacy tests. "If someone completes six grades and cannot read or write," said Ervin, "I say he shouldn't be allowed to vote."

"Is that what happens in North Carolina schools?" Kennedy snapped. "I just can't believe in this day and age, senator, that you are arguing that someone who's passed the sixth grade is illiterate. That's . . . unbelievable. Doesn't it disturb you when you read of Negroes being denied the right to vote on these grounds?"

Surely the most dramatic episode of his Attorney Generalship was the admission of the first Negro, James Meredith, to the University of Mississippi. Kennedy plotted carefully to avoid violence. He even rehearsed the admission ceremony with Mississippi Governor Ross Barnett, a staunch segregationist who wanted to look brave in front of his constituents. He would admit Meredith, Barnett said, only if he were threatened by pistols.

(left) "Finally, after two years in office, he argued his first case; from force of habit, he started at the top, before the Supreme Court." (center) May 6, 1961, University of Georgia Law Day Exercises. " 'I happen to believe that the 1954 decision [on school segregation] was right, but my belief does not matter — it is the law. Some of you may believe the decision was wrong. That does not matter. It is the law . . .' " (right) "Two weeks later, in Montgomery, Alabama, a mob of some 3000 whites, untroubled by the law or by local police, assaulted a group of Freedom Riders. Negroes were brutally beaten; so was John Seigenthaler from the Justice Department." This is a picture taken of Kennedy at his desk during the Montgomery violence.

"I will send the marshals that I have available . . . about twenty-five or thirty of them," said Kennedy, "and they will come with Mr. Meredith and they will arrive wherever the gate is and I will have the head marshal pull a gun and I will have the rest of them have their hands on their guns. . . . And then as I understand it he will go through and get in and you will make sure that law and order is preserved and that no harm is done to Mr. [Chief Marshal James] McShane and Mr. Meredith."

"Oh, yes," said Barnett.

Barnett reflected briefly. "General," he said, "I was under the impression that they were all going to pull their guns. . . . We got a big crowd here and if [only] one pulls his gun and we all turn, it would be very embarrassing. Isn't it possible to have them all pull their guns? Then they should point their guns at us and then we could step aside. . . ."

The more he heard, the less the Attorney General liked the plan. "To me, it is dangerous," he told Barnett, "and I think it has gone beyond the stage of politics."

The Attorney General's suspicions were justified. Barnett reneged on his agreement to maintain order, and the University of Mississippi campus exploded into violence. Two people died and 375 were injured; Barnett's state troopers watched without interfering. Through a bloody night, federal marshals resorted to tear gas to defend themselves, and Bobby ordered 3,000 army troops to the campus. He stayed in touch with his men, barricaded on the campus, by telephone.

"What's it like?" Bobby asked Ed Guthman at one point.

"Bob," said Guthman, "it's sorta like the Alamo."

"Well," said Kennedy, "you know what happened to those fellows."

Kennedy kept his poise, kept issuing directives, and, finally, the troops restored peace, and Meredith registered for classes. Later, Chief Marshal McShane was indicted by the State of Mississippi for his part in registering Meredith. McShane called Bobby who passed the phone to his brother, who asked if he could do anything for McShane.

"Yeah," said the Chief Marshal. "Get me a change of venue."

136

"Before he became Attorney General, Robert Kennedy's involvement and concern with civil rights was minimal . . . Always, in his statements and his actions, Bobby Kennedy proved himself a firm advocate; he won Negro admiration and ultimately the Negro vote."

"Where?" asked the President.

"How about the middle of Harlem?" said McShane.

Kennedy's tenure as Attorney General was marked periodically by civil-rights incidents—the tragedy of violence in Birmingham and the murder of Medgar Evers in Mississippi, the hope of the peaceful integration of the University of Alabama, and the reopening of schools to Negroes in Prince Edward County, Virginia—culminating in the Civil Rights Bill signed into law by Lyndon Johnson in 1964. Always, in his statements and his actions, Bobby Kennedy proved himself a firm advocate; he won Negro admiration and ultimately the Negro vote.

He was no less firm in his support of civil liberties. He condemned the radicals of the right; he had no sympathy, he said, for "those who, in the name of fighting communism, sow the seeds of suspicion and distrust by making false or irresponsible charges, not only against their neighbors but against courageous teachers and public officials. . . ." Some liberals would have rather he had spoken so forcefully a decade earlier.

His specific acts were even more encouraging, particularly his boldness in advocating the release from jail of Junius Scales, the only American ever imprisoned for having "knowingly been a member of the Communist Party," in violation of the Smith Act. Ironically, Scales did not begin his six-year sentence until after he had rejected the Communist Party. The FBI, the House Un-American Activities Committee, and the Senate Internal Security Subcommittee all argued that Scales be kept in prison because he had not named fellow communists. Bobby Kennedy ordered Scales pardoned.

"For the first time since the rise of McCarthyism," said Joseph Rauh, "an Attorney General has refused to treat a man's unwillingness to inform on others as a ground for withholding favorable government action in his case."

When the late A. J. Muste organized a Quebec-Washington-Guantanamo peace march, the State Department decided to block the pacifist's plan. In the

"Kennedy blended informality with hard work . . . lifted morale in the Justice Department." These pictures were taken at a party and cookout given for the staff and families of the Department.

Justice Department, Adam Walinsky worked on a memorandum saying that the State Department had no authority; the State Department ignored the memo and asked the Attorney General to sign a letter authorizing the stopping of the march.

"If an eighty-year-old man wants to walk eight hundred miles," said Kennedy, "I don't think that endangers the country. I won't sign it." (The Supreme Court later upheld Kennedy's position.)

"Then," Walinsky said later, "I knew he was my man."

Kennedy earned more liberal support with his proposals to guarantee that the impoverished criminal defendant would have free counsel in federal court, would not have to meet excessive bail requirements, and would have ample time to prepare his case. Kennedy won friends too by standing up to J. Edgar Hoover. He praised Hoover often, but he made certain that Hoover operated not independently, but within the Justice Department, under the Attorney General. And Kennedy directed the energies of the FBI, once concentrated so heavily on anticommunism, toward the more urgent war against organized crime.

The Attorney General was hardly perfect. He antagonized many of his supporters with the excesses of his drive to jail Jimmy Hoffa. He frustrated others with his ambivalent attitude toward wiretapping: "I am convinced that we need legislation to permit the use of wiretapping by law-enforcement officials," he wrote in his book, *The Pursuit of Justice*; "I do not believe in [wiretapping]," he wrote several pages later. Bobby compromised his civil-rights stature by sanctioning the appointment of a few federal judges who turned out to be rabid segregationists, and he did not help the cause of civil liberty when he unleashed FBI agents to awaken and question newspapermen in the middle of the night during the crisis over the rise in steel prices.

No one expected Bobby to be perfect. No one expected him to avoid all mistakes and miscalculations. The major surprise was that he did not attract greater criticism, considering the sensitivity of his position — he offered a most tempting target

Kennedy remained close to two older men; his father (left) with whom he visited at Cap d'Antibes on the Côte d'Azur in France, and Supreme Court Justice William Douglas (right) with whom he took a four-day camping trip in the Olympic National Park in the State of Washington.

139

for opponents of the Administration—and the multiplicity of his duties. On every issue, from political strategy to foreign affairs, the President sought his counsel; J.F.K. knew he could depend upon an honest opinion from Bobby, an opinion free from jealousy or selfish ambition. The President's subordinates, too, turned to Bobby; he was the ideal courier to carry messages between the President and his staff.

Inevitably, stories sprouted that Bobby was being groomed to take over the Presidency after John Kennedy completed a second term in 1968; the White House even received premature mail addressed to President Robert F. Kennedy. Daily, the two brothers spoke on the telephone; two or three times a week, they met at the White House. J.F.K.'s reliance upon Bobby became strikingly evident early in the Administration, after the abortive Bay of Pigs invasion, a disaster that convinced the President—and his brother—he could not accept absolutely the judgments of his military and intelligence experts.

The undermanned and underequipped invasion force never had a chance against Castro's troops, and Bobby sat in first on the death watch, then on the postmortems, unofficial and official. When word spread that Undersecretary of State Chester Bowles had opposed the invasion, Bobby Kennedy marched up to Bowles, poked a finger in his chest, and said, "I understand that you advised against this operation. Well, let me tell you as of right now, you did not. You were for it."

To investigate the Bay of Pigs fiasco, the President named a committee consisting of General Maxwell Taylor, Admiral Arleigh Burke, CIA Director Allen Dulles, and Bobby Kennedy. Bobby quickly assembled his top aides and told them that, for a while, he would be away from the Justice Department much of the time. "It'd be terrible," he said, "if the Department improves while I'm gone."

He spent his mornings examining documents and witnesses ("He brought out the fundamentals," said Maxwell Taylor, "and he saw the soft spots") at the CIA headquarters near his Virginia home, his afternoons at the White House, and his evenings catching up at the Justice Department. "What do you suppose the other Attorney Generals did with their time?" he asked an aide.

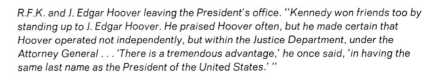

R.F.K. and J. Edgar Hoover leaving the President's office. "Kennedy won friends too by standing up to J. Edgar Hoover. He praised Hoover often, but he made certain that Hoover operated not independently, but within the Justice Department, under the Attorney General . . . 'There is a tremendous advantage,' he once said, 'in having the same last name as the President of the United States.' "

A month after the Cuban invasion, with the President off on a state visit to France and violence threatening the Dominican Republic, Bobby sat with Lyndon Johnson and Dean Rusk and directed United States ships to cruise by the Caribbean island. "Oh, yes," said John Kennedy later, explaining his brother's boldness in guiding foreign policy, "that's because I was out of the country."

Entrenched as a member of the National Security Council, a familiar figure slouched at Presidential conferences, Bobby shared with his brother the crisis over the Berlin Wall (to keep West Berlin free, said Bobby on television, the President "will use nuclear weapons"), the careful negotiations to produce a test-ban treaty, and, of course, the most harrowing experience, the Cuban missile crisis. It was Bobby, in ExComm, the President's inner circle, who argued down the suggestions for an immediate air strike upon the Cuban missile sites ("Pearl Harbor in reverse," he said), and it was Bobby who urged his brother to accept Premier Khrushchev's first conciliatory message agreeing to remove the missiles, and to act as though Khrushchev's second, more militant, message had never existed.

Bobby's fierce desire to help his brother drove him to spend time and energy raising the ransom for the Bay of Pigs prisoners, and it drove him, when J.F.K. wondered aloud how many Marines could march fifty miles in twenty hours, to march fifty miles himself. "He'd have finished," said Ed Guthman, "if he'd had to crawl."

Some of his trips were longer. In 1961, the President sent Bobby and Ethel to the celebration of the Ivory Coast's first year of independence; even though Bobby seemed a bit abashed by a display of bare-breasted folk dancers, he and his wife charmed the Africans with their fractured French. The next year, John Kennedy dispatched his brother and sister-in-law on a round-the-world goodwill tour, which prompted, before it began, two widely varying reactions. The Soviet Union asked to have Bobby visit Moscow, and Congressman John Lindsay wrote to the Secretary of State, "We question whether it is necessary for you and your office to be either burdened or embarrassed by free-wheeling foreign missions on the part of highly placed amateurs who do not have the background training, language ability, or capability to carry on the enormous burden of diplomacy. . . ."

Bobby rejected the invitation to Moscow, and the success of his trip repudiated Lindsay's criticism. In Japan, he flattered the women, swallowed the food (whale steak, seaweed), argued with the socialists, debated left-wing students, and won

(left) "To investigate the Bay of Pigs fiasco, the President named a committee consisting of General Maxwell Taylor, Admiral Arleigh Burke, C.I.A. Director Allen Dulles, and Bobby Kennedy." (right). October 15, 1962. A view of the White House one night during the Cuban Missile Crisis.

J.F.K., R.F.K., and Kenny O'Donnell at the White House.

(above) Ted Sorensen, McGeorge Bundy, Bob Kennedy, and Kenny O'Donnell waiting to see the President. (below) R.F.K. attending a meeting of the Executive Committee (ExComm) during the Cuban Missile Crisis. "It was Bobby, in ExComm, the President's inner circle, who argued down the suggestions for an immediate air strike upon the Cuban missile sites ('Pearl Harbor in reverse,' he said) . . ."

praise from both the press and the diplomatic corps. In Indonesia, he caught a piece of dried fruit in the face, lectured to some less violent students, discussed with President Sukarno the Dutch-Indonesian dispute over West New Guinea, and angered many Texans by saying, in response to a student's question, that the Mexican War "was not a very bright spot in our history." In India, he added Arthur Schlesinger to his entourage, inspiring Ethel Kennedy to write Ambassador John Galbraith, "Jackie Kennedy went to India and received silks, valuable stones, an elephant, and two tiger cubs, and we went to India and got Arthur Schlesinger."

In Italy, American correspondents presented Ethel with a motor scooter; she promptly drove into Roman traffic and sideswiped a Fiat. In Berlin, where Bobby called the Wall the "snake across the heart of your city," his speech drew a crowd of some 120,000 enthusiastic West Germans. In France, Bobby chatted for forty minutes with de Gaulle.

The trip cost its sponsor, the State Department, a total of $15,000, but it paid off in enormous goodwill and ample understanding. The State Department's own representative on the tour, a career man named Brandon Grove, was not, however, always understanding. Bred on protocol and promptness, Grove was,

In February, 1962, Kennedy went on a two-day visit to West Berlin. Shown here is part of the huge crowd of 120,000 that assembled to hear him speak, and a picture of him at the Berlin Wall with Mayor Willy Brandt.

Unlike his older brother, R.F.K. occasionally allowed himself to be photographed wearing a funny hat. Here he and G. Mennen Williams attend Independence Day celebrations in the Ivory Coast.

said one member of the Kennedy party, "a real cuff-snapper"; he invariably referred to the State Department as "*The* Department."

Grove's sense of efficiency was most deeply disturbed the day the Kennedys left Thailand. He told them to have their bags packed by eight p.m., before a dinner in their honor, so that they could depart immediately after dinner. Trapped in a hectic round of receptions, Ethel Kennedy changed her outfit three times and found no time to pack.

When Grove arrived at the dinner, he was furious. "It is chaos," he announced to John Seigenthaler. "Absolute chaos. Her bags were supposed to be packed by eight p.m. and it is now eight-o-five. They promised me they would have their bags packed by eight. It would take forty-five minutes to pack those bags if I had three manservants." Grove caught his breath. "John," he said, "I've had enough. They're going to have to learn that they're living in a real world with real people."

Seigenthaler slipped away from the dinner, went to the Kennedys' rooms, packed Ethel's bags for her, and made certain that everyone, and everything, reached the airport on schedule. Grove reached the airport still sulking. Bobby, who had been briefed by Seigenthaler, turned to Grove. "Well, Brandon," said the Attorney General, "what do they say in *The* Department?"

"Mr. Attorney General," said Grove, "I don't know if I'm going to speak to you, but I certainly will not speak to your wife."

When the entourage descended upon Rome, Ethel gave Grove a peace offering. She gave him a set of cuff links, one engraved "Real World," the other "Real People."

On the basis of his Asian-European trip, and a trip to Latin America later in 1962, Bobby Kennedy became convinced that too many people around the world simply had never been exposed to the American point of view. He urged that more prominent Americans be sent overseas to spell out United States policy and philosophy, and he urged too that ambassadors spend more time out of their embassies, touring their assigned countries and selling the United States to the people.

Attorney General, Presidential confidant, and roving ambassador, Bobby still managed to spend time at Hickory Hill, and the house in Virginia became almost legendary for its parties. There may have been no greater sign of status on the New Frontier than to have been pushed into the Kennedy swimming pool; Ethel Kennedy herself, Teddy Kennedy, Pierre Salinger, and Arthur Schlesinger headed the distinguished list. Ethel bubbled at Hickory Hill; one group named her "Homemaker of the Year," probably unaware of her total inability to prepare meals. But if she couldn't cook, Ethel charmed everyone with her informality, her spontaneity. Once, when Robert Frost came to lunch, Ethel had everyone at the table improvise poems, and Frost's, she reported, "were slightly better than the rest." When thirty guests gathered to honor the Duchess of Devonshire, Ethel said grace and adlibbed, "And, please, dear God, make Bobby buy me a bigger dining-room table."

With her husband, Ethel hosted the Hickory Hill seminars, at which a group of

Bobby delights children by skipping rope outside a Community Center for refugees in Hong Kong.

New Frontiersmen met once or twice each month to hear a distinguished visitor lecture on almost any subject apart from the daily operation of the government. The seminars were held, Schlesinger wrote, "to remind public officials that a world existed beyond their in-boxes."

Professors and psychiatrists, historians and humanists, came to the seminars, united in their intellectualism, and Ethel Kennedy, the relentless middle-brow, gamely did battle with them. Once she argued with Professor A. J. Ayer of London University when he derided abstract propositions; once she complained about the reading assigned for the seminars. "Terrible books to read—very heavy." Bobby, incidentally, polished his own reading ability with a course in speed reading that lifted him almost to his brother's sprinting level.

It was a vibrant, meaningful life for Bobby Kennedy, his life as the second-most-powerful member of the United States government, and then the assassin's bullet changed his life.

During the days immediately following the assassination, when he provided strength for friends and for family, particularly for the widow, Bobby Kennedy held up well. Then he began to crumble. Everyone around him noticed it. His eyes took on a hollow look. New lines entered his face. His clothes seemed to hang on him. He went on long walks, sometimes alone, sometimes with Brumus, sometimes with a friend or a reporter, and if he had always said little, he now said less. He cracked weak jokes. His hours on his job grew erratic, and he lost the ability to concentrate. "All my life," wrote Ed Lahey, a gifted reporter, "it seemed that the worst thing that could happen to you is to run out of room rent and eating money. But if you're rich, and young, with a fine family and a good job with an official limousine, life still can be like scratching your fingernail on a blackboard."

His friends worried about him and urged him to go away to ski or to sun. "Bobby should take a rest and go away and forget everything for a while," suggested Robert McNamara. "I'm afraid he'll get into a fight with Johnson."

The pictures on this and the previous page show Robert Kennedy walking around Hickory Hill with Brumus shortly after he learned of the President's assassination.

Bobby emerged slowly, easing his way back to reality, the fatalistic streak in him now fully developed. He indicated he would remain as Attorney General through the 1964 election and indicated he could sustain a working relationship with Lyndon Johnson ("I don't anticipate any problems"), yet his position had obviously changed. During Johnson's first major crisis, over Panama, Bobby was not called to the White House; J. Edgar Hoover stopped working through the Attorney General and reverted to reporting directly to the President.

Two months after his brother's death, Kennedy agreed to a diplomatic mission for Lyndon Johnson. To try to persuade Indonesia and Malaysia not to go to war over Northern Borneo, he visited Japan, the Philippines, Indonesia, and Malaysia; he won an agreement for at least a temporary truce.

Political pressures to bring Bobby the Vice-Presidential nomination began to build early in 1964, and, at first, if he did not openly encourage the grass-roots campaigns, he did little to stop them. Only a last-minute drive by the President brought Lyndon Johnson more Presidential votes in the New Hampshire primary than Bobby received as a write-in candidate for Vice President. Reports of a feud between John Kennedy's brother and John Kennedy's successor grew stronger, but Bobby denied them. "Our relations are friendly," he insisted. "They always have been. He has always been kind to me, to my family, and to Mrs. Kennedy. There is no substance to these reports."

Yet the reports persisted, spawning, with them, the feeling that Lyndon Johnson would not want Bobby Kennedy for his running mate. Kennedy's friends offered secondary political courses. Perhaps he could run for governor of Massachusetts—or even for senator from New York. "Sure they'd like him to run for the

—"Then he began to crumble. Everyone around him noticed it. His eyes took on a hollow look. New lines entered his face. His clothes seemed to hang on him."

Senate from New York," said one of Bobby's associates, more amused than annoyed. "They'd like him to try dog-catcher in Alaska too."

Bobby himself saw little point in invading a state he had not inhabited since childhood. "I don't think it's practical," he said. "It's better to get good people in the state to run." One day, as he drove through the Midtown Tunnel into Manhattan and wondered aloud whether he was going under the East River, he recognized how vulnerable he would be to a carpetbagger charge. "I'd tell them right out," he said. "If you want someone who has lived in New York all his life, vote for Ken Keating." Still he could not decide what he most wanted to do. He dismissed the idea of running for governor of Massachusetts; his younger brother Teddy was already a senator there. He offered to serve as ambassador to Vietnam, but Lyndon Johnson, who did not want to be charged with banishing Bobby from the country before the nominating convention, thanked him warmly and rejected the offer. He talked of teaching, or writing, but he remained intrigued, he admitted, by government.

"I'd like to harness all the energy and effort and incentive and imagination that was attracted to government by President Kennedy," Bobby told Ben Bradlee in an interview. "I don't want any of that to die. . . . If I could figure out some course for me that would keep all that alive and utilize it for the country, that's what I'd do."

Kennedy told Bradlee he did not expect to be tapped to run for Vice President. "Actually," he said, "I should think I'd be the last man in the world he would want . . . because my name is Kennedy, because he wants a Johnson Administration with no Kennedys in it, because we travel different paths, because I suppose some businessmen would object, and because I'd cost them a few votes in the South."

Yet Bobby never eliminated himself from consideration. He knew he would have great difficulty working with Johnson, he knew he would be stifled in the Vice Presidency, but he seemed to want, if not the job, at least the chance to turn it down. When his brother Teddy was seriously injured in a plane crash, Bobby announced firmly he would not run in New York for the Senate.

Still, even as The New York Times applauded Bobby's decision ("He had no legitimate claim to residence or to familiarity with problems of the state"), he looked more and more like a runner in search of a race. He made frequent speeches, invariably referring to his brother. "Coming back to West Virginia," he told one audience, "for a Kennedy is really like coming back home. There is close association with my family, particularly my brother." In Scranton, Pennsylvania, addressing The Friendly Sons of St. Patrick, he mentioned John F. Kennedy, then quoted a ballad memorializing Owen Roe O'Neill, a seventeenth-century Irish patriot:

"Oh, why did you leave us, Owen?
Why did you die?

". . . We're sheep without a shepherd,
When the snow shuts out the sky—
Oh! Why did you leave us, Owen?
Why did you die?"

Touring the South, the Midwest, the Far West, Bobby Kennedy spoke of civil rights, of war and peace, of his brother's contributions to humanity. Late in June, 1964, he went to West Germany to unveil a plaque in memory of John F. Kennedy, defended American participation in the war in Vietnam, and told his German audience, "The hope President Kennedy kindled is not dead but alive. . . . The torch still burns." He moved on to Poland, and he disrupted almost the entire nation with his antics, standing atop cars to wave to Polish citizens, singing to appreciative crowds "When *Polish* Eyes Are Smiling," announcing to a group of cheering students, "I am not a candidate for the Vice Presidency, but if you were in America and could vote for me, I would be." He told the Poles he was not running for President of the United States; he was running for Mayor of Cracow. The Mayor of Cracow laughed much more heartily than Lyndon Johnson might have.

Soon after Bobby returned from Europe, Johnson summoned him to the White House. They met on Wednesday, July 29, 1964, and the topic, as Kennedy had anticipated, was the choice of a Vice-Presidential candidate. "You have a bright future, a great name, and courage," said President Johnson, "but you have not been in government very long. I have given you serious consideration, but find it inadvisable to pick you."

Bobby, according to Johnson, swallowed hard.

*In Warsaw, Bob and Ethel
Kennedy stood on the top of a
car, sang "When Polish Eyes
Are Smiling," and "disrupted
almost the entire nation."*

149

September 12, 1964. The Kennedys stop in at the White House to say goodbye to President Johnson.

The two men discussed the Vice President's job ("I was miserable," said Johnson), the 1964 Presidential campaign (L.B.J. wanted Bobby to help run the campaign), and the selection of a new Attorney General. As he left, Bobby turned and said, "I could have helped you a lot."

"You are going to help," said the President.

Lyndon Johnson himself, and his aides, tried to persuade Bobby to announce that he did not want to be considered for the Vice-Presidential nomination, but Bobby, and his aides, turned down the chance to bow out gently. Johnson, who did not want to risk alienating the expanding Kennedy cult, decided on a shrewd, if transparent, maneuver to eliminate Bobby. On Thursday, July 30, the President called a press conference and revealed he had cut down his list of possible running mates. "It would be inadvisable," he reasoned, "for me to recommend to the convention any member of my Cabinet or any of those who meet regularly with my Cabinet." Robert McNamara, Adlai Stevenson, Orville Freeman, and Dean Rusk were swept aside with Bobby.

Kennedy retained his sense of humor. A few days later, at a school for Democratic congressional candidates, Bobby said, "I must confess I stand in awe of you. You are not members of the Cabinet, and you don't meet regularly with the Cabinet, and therefore you are eligible for Vice President." He smiled, and added, "I decided to send a little note to Cabinet members in general, saying, 'I'm sorry I took so many nice fellows over the side with me.'"

Now the Vice Presidency was out, the term as Attorney General was drawing to a close, and the elections of 1964 were fast approaching. Bobby Kennedy had to make a decision. He had to plot his future. The pressures upon him to run for the Senate from New York mounted daily. His brother-in-law, Stephen Smith, cheered by optimistic polls, urged him to run. Several New York Democratic and Liberal Party leaders, hungry for victory, urged him to run. Adlai Stevenson endorsed him. Very reluctantly, Mayor Robert F. Wagner of New York City endorsed him. Although *The New York Times* and the *Herald Tribune* and dozens of prominent

Reform Democrats openly told him to stay out of New York state, Bobby Kennedy knew the nomination was his if he wanted it.

Bobby was reluctant. He knew the charges of carpetbagger and opportunist that would be leveled against him. He knew that, even if he won, the Senate could not match in glamour and excitement the job he had filled. He knew that the campaign would not be an easy one, that he could conceivably lose and deeply damage his political potential. But he knew, too, above all else, that he had nowhere else to turn. His brother was up for reelection in Massachusetts. He could not expect to become Secretary of State or Secretary of Defense under Lyndon Johnson. And he did not want to surrender his place in public life.

On August 25, 1964, in an anticlimactic scene that had been preceded by leaks and even by the leasing of a $250,000 mansion on Long Island, Bobby Kennedy officially announced he wanted to become a United States senator from New York. He submitted his resignation to the President ("You will be back in Washington soon, where I can again call upon your judgment and counsel," wrote L.B.J.), accepted congratulations on his performance as Attorney General, attended a farewell rally staged by three thousand high school students grateful for his campaigns against dropouts and for better recreational facilities, parried questions about his own Presidential ambitions ("I think there's someone there . . . and I never see any statement that he is willing to move out"), and set off to run against the gentle, kindly, white-haired Republican who had endorsed him for Attorney General, Kenneth B. Keating.

Earlier that day, Kennedy spoke at the stadium of Washington's largely Negro Cardozo High School. The 3000 children, parents, and teachers gathered to express their feelings, as the two signs (among many) indicate.

CHAPTER EIGHT

ONE
IN
ONE HUNDRED

For sixteen minutes, he could not speak. For sixteen minutes, each time he sought to speak, thunderous waves of applause splashed over him. He swallowed hard. He hung his head. His eyes misted, and he fought back full tears. Finally, after sixteen emotional minutes in Atlantic City in 1964, after sixteen electric minutes in front of the Democratic National Convention that had nominated Lyndon Johnson for President and Hubert Humphrey for Vice President, Robert Kennedy began to speak, began to introduce a film honoring his dead brother. Sadly, softly, Bobby Kennedy quoted from *Romeo and Juliet*:

> "When he shall die,
> Take him and cut him out in little stars,
> And he will make the face of heaven so fine,
> That all the world will be in love with night,
> And pay no worship to the garish sun."

Five days later, *Romeo and Juliet* dissolved into *West Side Story*.

On its first ballot, despite some angry opposition, the New York State Democratic Convention overwhelmingly named Robert Kennedy to run for the United States Senate; the same day, the Liberal Party added its endorsement. Bobby's acceptance speeches formally thrust him into the race, but the heart of his campaign had been exposed in Atlantic City. He was running, consciously or not, as the heir to a dead President, and his emotional appeal could not be disputed.

Yet the thirty-eight-year-old candidate faced a frustrating struggle against a man so difficult to dislike as sixty-four-year-old Ken Keating. Keating's voting record, and his refusal to support Barry Goldwater for President, established him as a liberal Republican; his attendance record established him as a hard-working

153

". . . too blatant an appeal for sympathy . . . a suspicion that he was running too heavily on his brother's memory."

When he shall die
Take him and cut him out in
little stars,
And he will make the face of
heaven so fine,
That all the world will be in love
with night,
And pay no worship to the garish
sun.

senator; his insistent warnings about Soviet missiles in Cuba in 1962 established him as an aware senator. At the beginning of the campaign, at least, Bobby Kennedy could not attack Ken Keating on his record. Kennedy had to lean on his charisma, stress his potential, emphasize that he could be more than a capable senator, that he could be a great one.

Kennedy had to combat not only Keating, but dissent within his own party. Samuel Stratton, his disappointed rival for the Senate nomination, backed Kennedy, but in fiercely condemning the steamroller tactics that had decided the nomination, he had already given the Republicans ammunition. Charley Buckley, the autocratic boss of the Bronx, and Adam Clayton Powell, the boss of Harlem, embraced Kennedy as their chosen candidate, a gesture that, among certain Democratic factions, damaged Kennedy only slightly less than a joint endorsement from Gamal Abdel Nasser and James O. Eastland. Mayor Robert Wagner, the nominal leader of the Democratic Party in New York, supported Kennedy, but the faintness of his public praise reflected rather clearly the depth of his private bitterness.

Bobby and his advisers realized they could not count upon the Democratic State Committee for help, organizational or financial, and they built their own

machine, headed by brother-in-law Stephen Smith, powered by recruits from the
Department of Justice, by professional politicians from New York, even by a paid
gag writer. As the campaign progressed, the staff expanded; Peter Edelman and
Adam Walinsky waited a month before they were accepted on the campaign team,
then resigned from the Justice Department. Smith predicted that the campaign
might cost less than $1,000,000, but before he finished, he spent close to $2,000,000.
More than half the money went to an advertising agency, Papert, Koenig & Lois,
which poured most of its budget into television commercials, roughly one hundred
of them, ranging from twenty-second spots to thirty-minute films, aimed at
erasing the ruthless, illiberal McCarthy-Hoffa image that dismayed so many
New Yorkers, that prompted hostility from the local Americans for Democratic
Action and the local National Association for the Advancement of Colored People,
that led to the formation of Democrats for Keating — a vocal group including James
Baldwin, Gore Vidal, journalist I. F. Stone, and actor Paul Newman (who had once
been told by Kennedy that he should not narrate *Point of Order*, the fine docu-
mentary film that so effectively captured the sins of Joe McCarthy). Papert, Koenig
& Lois sought to project a new Kennedy image, of warmth, of concern, of states-
manship.

Kennedy's campaign started slowly. He had been running for two weeks, in fact,
before the telephones in his headquarters were operating properly. One night he
and several aides got lost on the streets of New York City. "We're on our way to a
meeting of the NAACP," Kennedy told a reporter. "That is, if the vaunted Kennedy
machine can find out where the meeting is being held."

He spent considerable time countering the carpetbagger charge. He admitted
he lacked the residency requirements to vote for himself in New York, but, in his
defense, he resorted to recent history (he had grown up in New York), to ancient
history (he pointed out that New York's first senator, Rufus King, had been im-

R. F. K.

*W. Averell Harriman and
Jacqueline and Robert Kennedy
receive delegates and guests of
the Democratic Convention in
Atlantic City, August, 1964.*

ported from Massachusetts), and to humor. In upstate New York, he said his voice sounded strange because he had a Long Island accent; on Long Island, of course, he pleaded an upstate accent. When a newsman told Kennedy he was taking a brief trip to Boston, Bobby snapped, "Never heard of it." When someone asked him privately why he didn't run in Virginia, he replied, "Because Charley Buckley and Adam Clayton Powell couldn't sponsor me in Virginia."

He also had to answer the charge of opportunism. "Strange as it may seem," he argued, "I just want to be a good United States senator." Once he said, "Let's assume that I'm using [New York] as a power base. . . . Let's just assume the worst. I can't go any place in 1968, we have a President . . . a good President until 1972. . . . I'll have to do an outstanding job in the Senate if people all over the country [are going to] demand that I be the [1972 Presidential] candidate. So I don't see how New York suffers."

(opposite page, top) R.F.K. at New York State Democratic Convention, September, 1964 To absolutely no one's surprise, he accepted the senatorial nomination. (opposite page, bottom) Nelson Rockefeller, Kenneth Keating, Jacob Javits, and Bob Kennedy share a hearty laugh in the reviewing stand at the Steuben Day Parade in New York City. Steuben Day is one of those occasions that seems to be noticed only during election campaigns. (left) Kennedy is swept in by acclamation at a meeting of the Sanitation Workers Union.

157

R.F.K.

Kennedy did not take immediately to the art of campaigning. His speeches seemed wooden in style and in content; almost never warm, rarely at ease, he monotonously ended his speeches with a quote from George Bernard Shaw: "Some people see things as they are and ask why. I dream of things that never were and ask why not." His habit of jabbing the air with his finger to emphasize a point, his endless references to President Kennedy, his decision to take young John F. Kennedy Jr. with him to visit the old family home in Riverdale—all seemed too blatant an appeal for sympathy; they reinforced a suspicion that he was running too heavily on his brother's memory.

And he did not handle the ethnic issue well. New Yorkers tend to vote in ethnic blocs; Bobby knew this, and he knew too that many Jews resented his association with McCarthy and his father's pre-World War II sentiments, and that many Italians resented what they considered the exaggerated zeal of his crusade against the Cosa Nostra. Bobby openly discussed the ethnic vote, which is a gross breach of political etiquette, yet had great difficulty playing to it, which is accepted political procedure. He seemed uncomfortable munching a *knish* or wearing a *yarmulke* among a Jewish crowd, and in an Italian neighborhood he committed the gaucherie of trying to eat pizza with a fork. During Rosh Hashanah, the Jewish New Year, he campaigned on Manhattan's West Side, a heavily Jewish area; his advisers told him he had to offer each Jewish voter New Year's greetings. "How can I?" said Kennedy. "How will I know which ones are Jewish?"

Because of the "Catholic issue" in 1960, J.F.K. never let himself be photographed with a group of nuns or priests. Clearly, R.F.K. feels there is no longer a "Catholic issue." This picture was taken outside St. Patrick's Cathedral during the 1964 campaign.

"... his decision to take young
John F. Kennedy, Jr., with him
to visit the old family home in
Riverdale..."

"Look at them," suggested one adviser, who was Jewish himself.

"It won't help," Kennedy confessed. "I can't tell that way."

His staff improvised. They assigned Al Blumenthal, a state legislator, to walk with Kennedy; each time a Jewish voter approached, Blumenthal would say "Now," and Kennedy would grab the voter's hand and say "Happy New Year."

The strategy worked perfectly until a policeman accidentally stepped on Blumenthal's foot. "Ow!" said Blumenthal, whereupon Bobby stuck out his hand and said "Happy New Year" to an understandably startled young Negro.

The Kennedy campaign dragged terribly in its early weeks, and by the end of September, the commanding lead Bobby had held in most prenominating polls had been dissipated. Keating, gaining sympathy, support, and momentum, moved

Three views of Kennedy, the campaigner, in October, 1964.

slightly in front, and Kennedy's camp began to worry. Then, suddenly, the campaign shifted; suddenly, Bobby Kennedy revived.

Some of his friends feel Kennedy finally shook the lingering effects of the assassination. Some feel he saw the precariousness of his position and recaptured his zest for a hard fight. Some feel an ill-advised Keating ploy—in late September he charged that Kennedy, as Attorney General, in approving the sale of a German company seized during World War II, had failed to prevent "a huge Nazi cartel" from sharing in the proceeds—spurred Bobby's competitive spirit and erased his reluctance to attack Keating personally. And some feel the size and fervor of the crowds he drew—especially in Buffalo, in Keating's home city of Rochester, and in tiny Glens Falls, where four thousand people, one-fifth the town's population, many of them in nightclothes, waited five hours to greet Bobby at 1 a.m.—stirred him to combat.

Whatever the causes, Kennedy perked up. He vilified Keating for implying pro-Nazism to him; he accused Keating of an unprincipled bid for ethnic votes. His speeches still lacked luster or significant content, but he touched more issues and his delivery improved slightly. He seemed less fearful of the masses who fought to touch him, to rip at his clothing, to press upon him copies of John Kennedy's *Profiles in Courage* for his autograph. His references to his brother grew less obvious, less irritating. At one question-and-answer session being filmed for a TV commercial, when someone asked him about the Warren Commission and its critics, Kennedy's composure surrendered to tears. He had the good taste to drop the scene from the commercial.

Above all, Bobby Kennedy had Barry Goldwater going for him. Although Keating did not endorse Goldwater, he would not say he was voting against him. Bobby thoroughly milked his rival's political discretion. Over and over, in a state thunderingly anti-Goldwater, Kennedy stressed he was the only senatorial candidate supporting Lyndon Johnson for President; the tactic won anti-Goldwater votes from Keating. A Conservative Party candidate, backing Goldwater, took away a smattering of votes at the opposite extreme.

Increasingly, Bobby spoke warmly of Lyndon Johnson, and Lyndon Johnson, in turn, spoke warmly of him. Politicians blessed the strange wedding with a simple analysis: Only a Johnson landslide, a distinct probability in New York, could guarantee a Kennedy victory.

The race turned Kennedy's way, but an element of risk remained. One difficulty lay in assessing the crowds Kennedy attracted; so many of his followers were teen-agers, and younger, that Bobby himself, only half in jest, called for an immediate reduction in the voting age—to six. Keating had to search for hands to shake. "Everywhere that Bobby goes," commented Eric Sevareid, "people are sure to gather; everywhere that people gather, Keating is sure to go." But no

162

one knew for certain whether people who wanted to look at Bobby also wanted to vote for him.

He finished his campaign boldly and effectively. His commercials flooded TV near Election Day. When a reporter uncovered a Fair Campaign Practices Committee letter criticizing Bobby for distorting Keating's position on the nuclear test-ban treaty, Kennedy pressured the committee to apologize for prematurely releasing the letter. The apology practically canceled the criticism. "An example," said a Kennedy aide, "of turning lemon into lemonade." When Keating purchased half an hour of prime television time to debate an empty chair—the two men had been unable to agree on ground rules for a TV confrontation—Kennedy showed up at Keating's studio a minute before air time and demanded admittance. Keating's aides blocked him. Kennedy, of course, neither expected nor really wanted to be admitted. He satisfied himself merely by puncturing Keating's argument that he was debating an empty chair because Kennedy feared him. Kennedy, and the newspapers, promptly revealed the scene outside the studio; the brash bit of showboating succeeded in making Keating look ridiculous. Kennedy began pulling away from Keating, and on Election Day, by some 628,000 votes, only a fourth of Lyndon Johnson's margin in New York State, Robert Kennedy won a seat in the United States Senate.

The senator-elect rushed off to Massachusetts to visit his hospitalized brother, Teddy, who had won reelection easily. "Hello," said Teddy, from his bed, "you ruthless power-hungry politician."

The Great Debate.

The sign and the smile were typical of what Robert Kennedy saw as he crisscrossed New York state during his 1964 campaign.

With his seat secured, Bobby, too, could afford to poke fun at himself. "I can't tell you how happy I am," he told the Women's National Press Club, "to be here representing the great state of—uh—uh—" Then he kidded his own ambitions. "I want to assure you," he said, "I have no Presidential aspirations—nor does my wife, Ethel Bird."

When the Senate convened, Bobby Kennedy ranked ninety-eighth in seniority, sixty-seventh among sixty-eight Democrats. He and Joe Tydings of Maryland sat alone in a special back row in the Democratic section. "I had better seats for *Hello, Dolly,*" Kennedy cracked.

Freshman senators traditionally serve quietly, watching their manners and their

164

elders, but Kennedy showed little respect for tradition. John Kennedy had waited five months to deliver his maiden speech, Teddy Kennedy sixteen months. Bobby waited three weeks. Then he offered an amendment extending Appalachian anti-poverty aid to thirteen New York counties, a move he had not discussed with either New York's Governor Nelson Rockefeller or New York's senior Senator Jacob Javits. In sharp contrast to his brother Teddy, who played the game by the un-written rules, deferred to his seniors, and earned considerable popularity within the Senate, Bobby established himself quickly as a maverick. He admitted he was impatient with the pace of the Senate, frustrated by its formality. As the junior member of committees and subcommittees to which he was appointed, Kennedy could ask questions only after other senators had asked theirs. Most senators questioned calmly, from their seats. Bobby prowled about, playing the role of the investigator-prosecutor once more.

He did not hesitate to voice his differences with the Johnson Administration. In his fifth month in office, Kennedy disputed the Administration's intervention in the Dominican Republic crisis. The following month, he delivered a major speech on nuclear proliferation despite hints that Johnson wanted him to wait until after a Presidential speech on the topic. Kennedy urged that Communist China participate in discussions to stop the spread of nuclear weapons; the White House viewed the speech coolly. In July, 1965, Kennedy spoke out on the war in Vietnam, but he revised his prepared text to delete criticism of the Presi-dent's efforts and to insert support for strong military action in Vietnam. Although he argued that political actions, not military ones, offered the key to stability, Bobby cropped his remark that "victory in a revolutionary war is not won by es calation, but by de-escalation." The White House pronounced the amended tex "helpful."

Neither Kennedy nor Johnson seemed eager to break openly with the other. In the first issue of *R.F.K. Reports*, a news etter for his constituents, Kennedy dis-couraged persistent reports of a feud by placing on the front page a picture of himself shaking hands with the President.

New York's Senators Kennedy and Javits together in the Senate Gallery in the Capitol.

Kennedy visits his
brother's grave shortly
before taking his seat in
the United States Senate.

Matthew Maxwell Taylor Kennedy, number nine,
is baptized at St. Patrick's. Joseph and Kathleen
Kennedy serve as godparents while Father,
Aunt Jacqueline, and Cousins Caroline and
John look on.

(top) Two distinguished members from New York. This picture was taken on April 15, 1965, in the East Room of the White House before Mr. Powell moved south.
(bottom) R.F.K. peers out of a helicopter through the smog and pollution during a trip to New York with Secretary Stewart Udall.

Kennedy speaking at night in Harlem. He urged teenagers to participate in local programs of the anti-poverty drive.

Senators Ribicoff and Kennedy during a subcommittee hearing on auto safety.

If Kennedy was not the usual freshman senator, he still impressed some of his colleagues. "With all due respect to the kind of President Jack turned out to be," said one senator, "Bob is going to be a hell of a lot better senator. He's a harder worker than his brother was when he was here." Kennedy worked for passage of an amendment granting voting rights to Puerto Ricans literate in Spanish, helped to keep open two Veterans Administration hospitals in New York, and tried unsuccessfully to save the Brooklyn Navy Yard.

His interests, of course, extended far beyond his constituency. Once Bobby testified on behalf of a bill to curb interstate shipment of firearms; a model of the rifle used by Lee Harvey Oswald was on display in the hearing room. Another time, during a subcommittee hearing on auto safety, Kennedy's questioning prodded James M. Roche, the president of General Motors, to reveal that GM, with a profit of 1.7 billion dollars in 1964, spent only $1,250,000, less than one percent, on safety.

Bobby, like J.F.K. before him, found only limited time to involve himself in the politics of the state he represented. His few brushes with New York Democratic politics were not rewarding. Early in 1965, after the Johnson sweep carried the Democrats to control of both houses of the state legislature, a leadership struggle broke out between pro-Wagner and pro-Kennedy forces. The Wagner group was outnumbered, but neither side had decisive strength. After a tedious, almost comical battle that seriously delayed the work of the legislature, the Republicans abruptly lined up with the Wagner men and elected the anti-Kennedy forces leaders of the legislature. The Democrats appeared foolish. "It's going to be very, very difficult to resurrect the party," said Bobby. When he later denounced the new leaders for substituting "patronage" for "excellence" in their appointments, and the leaders in turn angrily denounced his interference, Kennedy deepened the divisions within the party. He did not enhance his stature later in the year either, when, after Bob Wagner withdrew from the race, he did not endorse any one Democratic primary candidate to oppose Republican John Lindsay for mayor of New York. Lindsay won, giving the Republicans three of the four major political positions in New York State. Bobby tangled with all three Republicans—Lindsay, Rockefeller, Javits—but even though he sometimes upstaged Javits with advance knowledge of federal grants in the state, he seemed happier with his senatorial colleague than with the governor, whom he did not like, or the mayor, whom he did not respect.

Despite his duties in the Senate and New York—a mild burden after his chores as Attorney General—the freshman senator managed to relax occasionally in his usual energetic style. Early in the spring, he decided to climb a 13,900-foot mountain in the Yukon, the tallest untamed peak in North America. "I've never climbed a mountain before," he confessed. "I hate heights." But he chose to challenge the peak because it had been renamed Mount Kennedy, after his brother. "I think he wants to take his mind off the fact that he's not an astronaut," Ethel Kennedy suggested. He had experts to guide him, to shield him from strain and disaster, but his feat still demanded courage. At one treacherous point, he recalled his

"He admitted he was impatient with the pace of the Senate . . ."

(top and bottom) Two views of
Kennedy campaigning for Abe
Beame against John Lindsay
during the 1965 New York City
mayoralty race. Both Beame
and Kennedy were losers.

(opposite page — top left) Bob Kennedy and Jim
Whitaker haul a towline before climbing Mt.
Kennedy in the Yukon, previously the highest
unclimbed peak in North America. " 'I never
climbed a mountain before. I hate heights.' "
(top right) in November, 1965, the Kennedy's led
a large party through South America. Here R.F.K.
is shown speaking to a street crowd in Brazil and
(below) visiting a barrio in the same country.

mother's classic advice, "Don't slip, dear," and he wondered, "What am I doing here?" But he reached the peak and marked it with three PT-109 tie clasps and a copy of J.F.K.'s inaugural address. Most professional mountain climbers were unmoved by Kennedy's daring, but most sea-level voters found it far more impressive than his judgment.

Late in 1965, Bobby took another hazardous journey, a trip to Latin America, and reporter Andrew Glass shared and recorded the hazards. Greeted by adulation and unsolicited Presidential endorsements almost everywhere, determined to inspect poverty first hand, Kennedy seemed to relish most the dangers of the trip. In Chile, ignoring a warning to avoid the university, he stood up to a barrage of eggs and garbage from howling communist students, listened to cries of "Go home, go home, you Yankee son of a whore," and argued, unheard, for the right of free expression. In Brazil, he took a seaplane into the Amazon jungle, shifted to a dugout canoe, and as he waded through menacing waters, cheerfully mimicked a prominent television voice: "It was impossible to pinpoint the exact time and place when he decided to run for President. But the idea seemed to take hold as he was swimming in the Amazonian river of Nhamunda, keeping a sharp eye peeled for man-eating piranhas." Dramatic pause. "Piranhas have never been known to bite a U. S. senator."

During his second year in the Senate, Kennedy reached a peak of personal popularity, a peak remarkable because he rarely catered to the national consensus. Eager to prove himself an influential senator, he aimed his words and actions more at the country than at the Senate itself. Equipped with a stable of experts and consultants to shape his speeches and his thinking, he entrenched himself to the left of the Johnson Administration and spoke out on the vital issues facing the country. In a speech on Vietnam, he called for the inclusion of the Viet Cong in a post-truce government; "putting a fox in a chicken coop," argued Vice President Humphrey. Bobby went to the University of Mississippi, the bloody battlefield of his Attorney General days, and welcomed by a cheering crowd of sixty-five hundred, he advocated "a society in which Negroes will be as free as other Americans." He struggled unsuccessfully to block budget cuts in the war on poverty and in other Great Society programs; and he delivered to the Senate a massive speech on Latin America, urging more land reform, recommending greater tolerance of youthful left-wing nationalists, warning that the United States should not automatically rush to support Latin Americans for "whom the cry of 'communism' is only an excuse for the perpetuation of privilege." He proposed that the United States initiate steps to bring Communist China into the United Nations to facilitate "greater dialogue." And in the middle of 1965, Bobby darted off on another of his trips, this one to South Africa, where he observed the evils of *apartheid*, met with Chief Albert Luthuli, the house-imprisoned leader of half a million South African blacks, then came home to author a magazine article, "Suppose God Is Black." The title certainly had shock value; so did one sentence within the article. "My father," Kennedy wrote, "finally left Boston, Massachusetts, because of the signs on the wall that said, 'No Irish Need Apply.'" The senator protested too

The pictures on these pages attest to the tremendous response that Kennedy received in Latin America — a response he attributed to the reservoir of good feeling for the United States, to the Alliance for Progress, and to the memory of his dead brother. Reporters along with him on the trip said also that the people were responding to Robert Kennedy directly and to his obvious interest in and concern for their welfare.

ong live the
lliance for Pro_
ress. great lega_
y of John F.
Kennedy.
obert Kenn
elcome to Th
The teachers of
Zurite appreciate the
help of Uncle Sam
to our communities.

In June, 1966, the Kennedys went to Africa. In Nairobi, R.F.K. is greeted by a group of women whose views about the American role in Vietnam apparently correspond to his own.

much; his father left Boston, in a private railroad car, in search of millions.

As he bathed himself in national and international politics, Kennedy immersed himself deeper in New York, too. Working sometimes out of his official six-room suite in a post-office building in Manhattan, sometimes out of his own $68,000 apartment in the United Nations Plaza, he enlisted dozens of young lawyers, educators, and businessmen, all happy to tie themselves to the senator's rising star, and put them to work on a broad variety of projects—tutorial programs for the emotionally disturbed in New York City schools, new parks in the Bronx, attracting and stabilizing industry in Brooklyn's Negro ghetto of Bedford-Stuyvesant. Most of his parttime recruits, like most of his staff, became fiercely loyal supporters.

On the New York political front, he scored his first notable success. When the regular Democratic and Republican organizations banded together to support

The childrens' signs bear out R.F.K.'s conclusions.

These pictures taken in Tanganyika, Tanzania, and South Africa again illustrate the special feeling the Kennedys reserve for young people everywhere — a feeling that is quite clearly reciprocated.

(opposite page, top) "Here, kitty. Nice kitty." The Kennedys with Emperor Haile Selassie and a palace pet.
(opposite page, bottom) In South Africa with Nobel Prize winner Albert Luthuli.
In Kenya with President Jomo Kenyatta.

Bobby "put his full prestige behind an insurgent candidate [for Manhattan Surrogate], Supreme Court Justice Samuel Silverman. When Silverman decisively defeated Arthur Klein in the Democratic primary, the victory, beyond question, was Bobby's; few voters knew anything about Silverman or Klein, and cared less."

Senators Kennedy and Javits campaigning in New York City for a civilian review board to weigh citizens' complaints against alleged police misconduct. ". . . but he campaigned without great enthusiasm, and the review board lost, hurting Mayor John Lindsay more than Kennedy."

New York Supreme Court Justice Arthur Klein for the post of Manhattan Surrogate, a job rich in patronage, the Reform Democrats and the Liberals complained bitterly of a deal. The dissidents persuaded Bobby to share their fight, and once he did, he put his full prestige behind an insurgent candidate, Supreme Court Justice Samuel Silverman. When Silverman decisively defeated Klein in the Democratic primary, the victory, beyond question, was Bobby's; few voters knew anything about Silverman or Klein, and cared less. With this fight, with his speeches, and with his perfect—by Americans for Democratic Action standards—voting record in the Senate, Kennedy converted many New York liberals to his side. "I've been impressed," said Carey McWilliams, the editor of *The Nation* and, in 1964, a Democrat for Keating. "He's been . . . attentive to the problems of the city and state. I'd work for him now."

Kennedy campaigned vigorously across the country in the 1966 congressional and gubernatorial elections. Here he is flying to Chicago to help Senator Paul Douglas.

179

Within the Senate, Kennedy occupied a strange position. Few people risked attacking him openly ("I treat him," said one senator, "the same way I'd treat any future President"), but even though he insisted he was not pursuing any Presidential ambitions ("If I tried to . . . I'd be a basket case in three months"), many resented him.

Kennedy obviously considered himself a transient in the Senate, obviously used the Senate mainly as a platform for his speeches and as a place to gather his strength and forces for an ultimate political drive. "They only take about one vote a week here," he said, "and they never can tell you in advance when it is going to be so you can schedule other things. If I am not going to be working here, I want to go somewhere I can do something."

"Bobby is not a senator's senator," said one colleague. "He understands very well the limitations of achieving a national identity if you keep your nose close to the legislative grindstone. I would call Bobby a hit-and-run senator. He'll come into a committee room where the TV cameras are, take a slug at General Motors, and leave. The drudgery of writing and shepherding a bill is left to someone else."

"Bobby is an existential politician," said another senator. "Wherever the action is, he goes. Like Capetown, where he denounced *apartheid*, and Cracow, where he talked about freedom. His interests are outside the Senate. I would call him a first-act politician. You know it's easy to write the first act. And it's relatively easy to write the third act. Lyndon Johnson was a good third-act man. He liked to wrap things up. But it's the second act that is toughest to write. In Congress, that's where the drudgery and hard work come."

Kennedy could not guide a bill neatly to passage. He could not often sway his colleagues' votes. He could not trade senatorial favors. But he could, above all other senators, exercise a magic appeal to the electorate. His charisma seemed stronger than ever—the memory of John Kennedy brighter than ever—and all over the United States people wanted to see him, to hear him, and to vote for him, even people who did not share his views. He was, by the end of the summer of 1966, the most popular Democrat in the United States, running in all polls well ahead of Lyndon Johnson, far ahead of Hubert Humphrey.

Candidates for Congress, for the Senate, and for governorships sought his endorsement and his presence in their campaigns. Governor Pat Brown of California, challenged by Ronald Reagan, said that given a choice between Lyndon Johnson and Bobby Kennedy to speak for him, he would pick Bobby. Kennedy agreed to speeches in roughly a dozen states, and everywhere, in West Virginia, in Iowa, in Ohio, he drew stunning and admiring crowds. Once, in Cincinnati, when he stood atop a Cadillac and the roof caved in, he said, "I can tell you right now this one'll cost three hundred dollars. I've done it before." National magazines wrote of "The Bobby Boom," of "The Bobby Phenomenon," of "The Making

(opposite page, top) Another example of the close rapport that exists between the President and Senator Kennedy. (bottom) Kennedy's energetic and sincere efforts did not save Paul Douglas from defeat by Charles Percy (standing next to Douglas is Mayor Daley of Chicago).

R. F. K.

(opposite page, top) Kennedy's less than energetic efforts did nothing to save Frank O'Connor from defeat by Nelson Rockefeller. (bottom) In California, Kennedy was met by mixed reactions and Governor Brown was crushed by Ronald Reagan.

of President Robert Kennedy," and few people doubted that someday Bobby Kennedy would live in the White House.

And then, in the final months of 1966, his popularity began to diminish.

Little things went wrong, and big things. Bobby failed to come up with his own candidate for governor of New York—his first choice, businessman Sol Linowitz, refused to run—and Frank O'Connor won the Democratic nomination almost by default. O'Connor's plodding disastrous campaign against Nelson Rockefeller did not help Kennedy's prestige. Elsewhere around the country, several candidates he had backed were defeated; in Florida, the man he had strongly supported in the Democratic primary won the gubernatorial nomination, but lost the general election to a Republican. Kennedy endorsed a proposed civilian-review board to weigh complaints against the police in New York City, but he campaigned without great enthusiasm, and the review board lost, hurting Mayor John Lindsay more than Kennedy. Bobby, of course, did not especially mind seeing Lindsay suffer;

R. F. K.

little warmth flowed between them. Once, when Kennedy and Javits came to break-fast at the mayor's mansion to discuss the review board, one of the mayor's aides arranged, without the mayor's knowledge, for an expensive and exotic restaurant to cater the breakfast.

After pâté de foie gras for an appetizer, followed by caviar omelettes, with the main course still to come, Kennedy stared at the mayor and asked, innocently, ''Do you eat like this all the time?''

Robert Price, the deputy mayor, counterpunched. "You should see how we eat," said Price, "when we have friends here."

Late in 1966, extending into 1967, two major controversies erupted and damaged Kennedy deeply. One was an argument over the use of bugging devices by the FBI during Kennedy's tour as Attorney General. J. Edgar Hoover coolly insisted that Kennedy had sanctioned electronic eavesdropping; Kennedy insisted that he had no knowledge of such practices. Each man produced documents and wit-

nesses and fought his case furiously through the newspapers. While neither man really won, only Kennedy lost. Bobby never had a chance. If he had admitted knowledge of bugging, he would have hurt himself with liberals; by denying knowledge, he looked like a lax administrator. Besides, by conceding that he did approve telephone wiretapping in national security cases, he antagonized liberals, and merely by feuding with Hoover, he antagonized conservatives.

The Manchester affair, overlapping with the bugging battle, made Bobby look even worse. Cast as censor and tyrant—roles surely confirmed in part, if not in whole, by his actions—Bobby also emerged as a man using the story of the death of his brother as a sword in his personal duel with Lyndon Johnson. The indictment may be too severe; perhaps, as Bobby's associates indicate, he did object to unjust criticism of Johnson in *The Death of a President*. Yet his comments to Manchester about the telephone calls from Dallas on the day of the assassination, those comments alone, were sufficient to paint an unpleasant portrait of Lyndon Johnson. Bitterness came through clearly enough to show Kennedy as a man at war with his President.

The Bobby Kennedy of 1967 did not seem strikingly different from the Bobby Kennedy of 1966, but almost everything he touched turned to dross. A dispute arose over the Harvard Institute of Politics, a charge that it was merely a shadow cabinet for Bobby Kennedy, and Bobby came out the villain. He spoke on Vietnam, voicing disagreement with the national majority, and now, perhaps because everything he said was set against the background of the Manchester battle, he aroused more enmity than he had with all his earlier dissenting speeches—approving blood donations for the Viet Cong, advocating the entry of Red China into the United Nations, calling for a realistic approach to internal revolutions in Latin America. On a less cosmic scale, he forced the resignation of the crafty Democratic leader of Manhattan, Raymond Jones, a move that might once have been interpreted as enlightened, but now, instead, raised familiar cries of ruthlessness. Even so moderate a step as a mild indication that he favored reforms in the New York State abortion laws injured Kennedy; it angered Catholics and failed to win him converts among the liberals who distrusted him. He traveled extensively in New York state, and young people still crowded around him and gaped and sighed and squealed, but his broader appeal had unmistakably faded. Critics charged, with some justification, that he had been overexposed, that the public had tired of him, at least temporarily. In the polls, he fell behind Lyndon Johnson as the favorite among Democrats and independents.

The change in one year in Robert Kennedy's stature was dramatic. In the middle of 1966, he actually seemed to believe that, somehow, he might successfully wrest the 1968 Presidential nomination from Lyndon Johnson, that he might be President of the United States in 1969.

But, within twelve months, by the middle of 1967, Bobby Kennedy was wondering whether he would ever have the chance even to run for President.

"Little things went wrong, and big things . . . by the middle of 1967, Bobby Kennedy was wondering whether he would ever have the chance even to run for President."

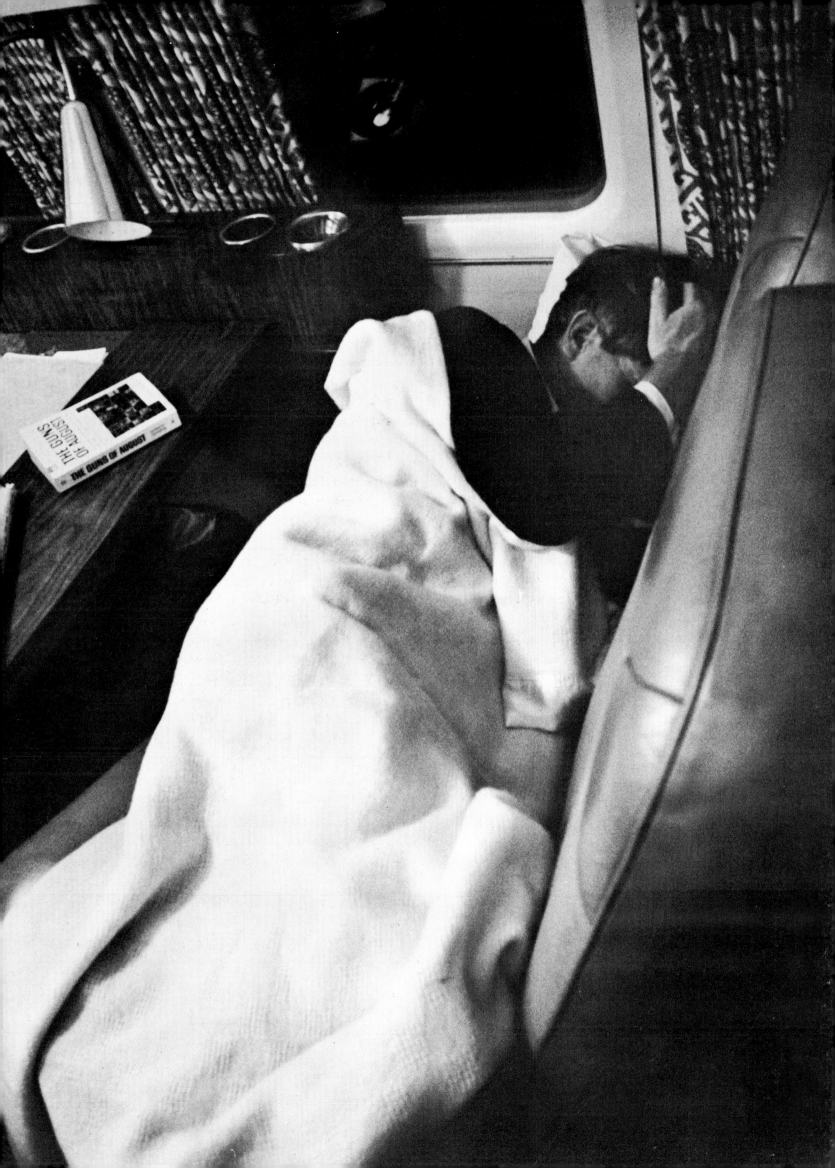

CHAPTER NINE

ALL THE WAY WITH R.F.K.?

Robert Francis Kennedy, one of his friends has suggested, could be the Adlai Stevenson of the 1970s, which is, at once, both a beautiful and terrible thing to say about any politician. Adlai Stevenson gave the United States in the 1950s an articulate voice of sanity. He was a thoughtful man, a compassionate man. He was also a loser.

The surface differences between Kennedy and Stevenson, of course, could hardly be more striking. Stevenson's cerebrations led him often to indecision; Kennedy's instincts lead him often to impetuosity. Stevenson savored a neatly turned phrase; Kennedy prefers a precise phrase. Stevenson found the prospect of being President awesome; Kennedy views the job without illusions or qualms. Stevenson hated to make enemies; Kennedy enjoys the number and nature of his foes. Stevenson, who was not a shy man, offered himself to the public reluctantly; Kennedy, who is shy, thrives upon recognition and acceptance.

Yet the bonds between the two men are clear. Stevenson wanted to be President, but not quite so much as he wanted to be reasonable; Kennedy wants to be President, but not quite so much as he wanted his brother to be President. Stevenson refused to mask his egghead image, which unsettled many voters; Kennedy refuses to abandon his youthful, long-haired image, which irritates many voters. Stevenson would not compromise his principles merely to gain votes; Kennedy will not shy away from unpopular stands to seek the majority's favor.

Bobby Kennedy could indeed be the Stevenson of the 1970s, the uncrowned spokesman of an elite minority, but one simple, significant difference separates the two men. Stevenson knew, beyond any doubt, that his unwillingness to adjust to the electorate could cost him the Presidency; Kennedy may suspect, with no great degree of certainty, that his unwillingness to adjust to the electorate could win him the Presidency. Stevenson functioned in a postwar decade that hungered for stability, for comfort, for the predictability of an Eisenhower, but Kennedy lives

189

"Lyndon Johnson is his main enemy . . . The feeling now is that Johnson wants Bobby never to be President and will do everything in his power, which is considerable, to keep him from the White House."

in a period of tremendous instability, of enormous upheaval. The structures of governments, of warfare, and of society are changing, a sign that the structure of politics must be changing, too. Kennedy's tactics could be perfectly suited to the new politics. If this is true, his critics might call him calculating, his friends might call him insightful. More reasonably, Kennedy is charting his course only intuitively.

The shift toward a new politics provides, at least, one logical explanation of Kennedy's current stance. Unlike Stevenson, he is not a good loser. And, more than Stevenson, he is a practical politician, a totally contemporary politician, skilled at using the communications media, at orchestrating the news, at projecting the image he wishes to project. Bobby Kennedy would not willingly choose a course that would destroy his chances for victory.

"Strangely, the relationship between Kennedy and Humphrey is a genuinely pleasant one."

Still he has selected a risky course, a gambler's course. He is wooing fickle audiences. He appeals to the young, who have always grown conservative with age. He appeals to the intellectuals, who scorned John Kennedy until 1960, who turned on Adlai Stevenson after 1960. He appeals to the impoverished, who can be dazzled by a hero, by an Eisenhower. He is the logical beneficiary of the anti-war vote, which evaporates if the war ends. He has followers who applaud his acts, but distrust his motives. A solid and sizable core of Kennedy voters certainly exists — a dominant share of the Negro vote and the Catholic vote, a substantial share of the female vote, the people who voted for John Kennedy and cherished him, some people who did not vote for John Kennedy and now, infected by a national post-assassination guilt, want to make amends to his brother — but much of his support is precarious, and time could erode the bright memory of his brother. If he has gambled poorly, if the young outgrow their enthusiasm for him, if the poorly fed and poorly educated fail to appreciate his efforts, or if the country simply decides

In Washington, some observers feel that Bobby, who has made many enemies, will eventually decide to step aside for Teddy, who so far has made none. Today, however, that seems highly unlikely.

191

"He is driven now by a curious mixture of fatalism and impatience. He admits he cannot hurry the political timetable. He knows that in 1976, he will be only fifty, younger than most Presidents at the time of their election, and that in 1984, if the world survives to the Orwellian year, he will be fifty-eight, hardly ancient by

to try the Republican Party for a change, Bobby Kennedy can easily become a Stevensonian figure, a man almost, but never President.

The closer one comes to Kennedy, the more one recognizes the difficulty of his quest for the Presidency. He is surrounded on all political sides by strong and dedicated enemies. One obvious sign is the rash of anti-R.F.K. books and magazine articles; anti-J.F.K. literature did not really flourish until he became President. The resistance to Bobby from the right does not damage him greatly; the currents flowing against him within his own party are more subtle, and more crucial, because, in his fight to become President, his first, and probably more hazardous, struggle is to be nominated.

Even though several promising young Republicans have emerged nationally, with justifiable hopes of upsetting the Democratic Party in 1972 or even in 1968, the odds are that Bobby could win a race for the Presidency—partly because Democrats usually win, partly because he possesses the weapons essential to a

Presidential standards. But even as he concedes the futility of pressing too hard too soon for the Presidency, he keeps looking for the proper moment. He seems to suspect that his popularity will rise again, possibly for reasons beyond logic, and when and if he finds the proper moment, he will act."

successful campaign — if he could get the nomination. But to secure the nomination, he must overcome small enemies — for instance, Mayor Sam Yorty of Los Angeles, who argues, "He's trying to ride on his brother's fame and his father's fortune" — and large enemies.

Lyndon Johnson is his main enemy. "We're not on the same wave length," Bobby has said, but the problem is more complex. Johnson is an excessively sensitive man, and he resents, bitterly, what he considers Kennedy's ingratitude and Kennedy's sniping. Once Johnson maintained that he would never block Bobby from the Presidency, but a year later, asked privately whether he would, under any circumstances, accept Kennedy as his running mate in 1968, L.B.J. snapped he "wouldn't take Bobby if he were the last Democrat on earth."

"I have lived through too many conflicts to be impressed by the Kennedy-Johnson feud," Larry O'Brien says. O'Brien is surely an astute politician, astute enough to be correct — or astute enough to state a generality that even he does

193

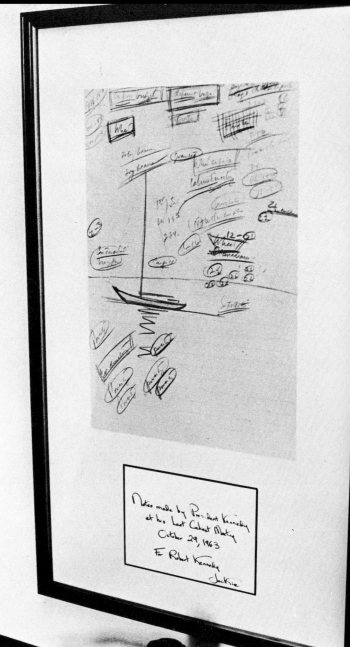

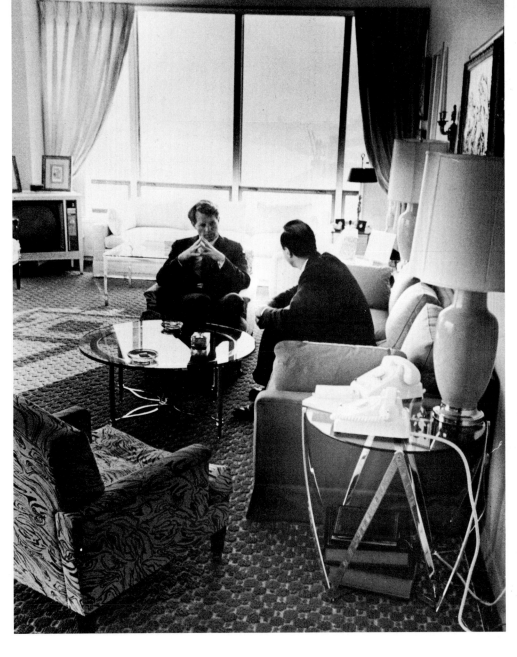

(opposite page, top left) Behind Kennedy, in his Washington office, is a portrait of his brother, Joseph P. Kennedy, Jr., who was killed in World War II. (opposite page, top right) Framed and hanging on R.F.K.'s office wall are "Notes made by President Kennedy at his Last Cabinet Meeting, October 29, 1963." The notes were given to Bob Kennedy by Jacqueline Kennedy. The word "poverty" was written many times and circled by the President. (opposite page, bottom) Bob Kennedy with two of his closest non-staff advisors, William vanden Heuvel and Richard N. Goodwin. (left) The living room of the Kennedy's New York apartment, which is a short distance away from the United Nations and overlooks the East River.

not fully believe. Kennedy, a politician too, will support Lyndon Johnson in 1968 and will campaign for him, but this token display of inescapable party loyalty will not erase the President's bitterness. The feeling now is that Johnson wants Bobby never to be President and will do everything in his power, which is considerable, to keep him from the White House. Johnson's own candidate, for the present, is his Vice President, Hubert Humphrey.

Strangely, the relationship between Kennedy and Humphrey is a genuinely pleasant one. Each often pounces upon the other's remarks—after all, Humphrey must, in his job, defend the President—but the rancor of the 1960 West Virginia primary has given way to mutual affection and respect. Humphrey does not hesitate to phone Kennedy (one afternoon early in 1967, Bobby's office took, in rapid succession, direct calls, not through secretaries, from Humphrey, Ambassador Arthur Goldberg, and Johnny Carson), and Kennedy does not hesitate to consult Humphrey. Bobby knows that Humphrey, when he learned of the death of John F. Kennedy, put his head on his desk and cried for half an hour; with this knowledge, Bobby could never enthusiastically attack the Vice President. Bobby realizes, somewhat sadly, that he has usurped much of Humphrey's left-of-center constitu-

Robert and Caroline Kennedy at the dedication of the John F. Kennedy memorial at Runnymede, England. (opposite page) March 15, 1967. Richard Cardinal Cushing blesses the permanent gravesite of President Kennedy and his two deceased children during the private reinterment service at Arlington National Cemetery. Left to right are: Theodore Sorensen, Mrs. Edward Kennedy, Robert Kennedy, President Johnson, a Secret Service officer, Mrs. John F. Kennedy, and Edward Kennedy.

ency, and he does not admire the liberals for their hasty loss of faith in Humphrey. Still Bobby is not above kidding his rival. Once, when he received a letter asking for a copy of his "inaugural address," Kennedy sent the letter to Humphrey with the message, "I just wanted you to know how my mail was running." Humphrey, a gentle man who wants to be President too, who has an easy confidence in himself and in humanity, does not attack Bobby personally. "The name of Kennedy

means a lot, let's face it," Humphrey has said. "But it's also fair to say they carry their honored name well. . . . The senator does enjoy immense popularity, and all I can say is that thank goodness he is a Democrat."

In April, 1967, for the first time, Hubert Humphrey overtook Bobby Kennedy in Democratic popularity polls, a development that had to impress both men. Yet Kennedy recognizes the erratic nature of political popularity. He is no more depressed by his sagging showings in the polls of 1967 than he is elated by the posters blaring, "Bobby in '68," "Bobby in '72," "Bobby Anytime," or by the unauthorized committees boosting him for President in 1968.

Bobby Kennedy may once have dreamed of running for President in 1968, but he realizes now that this is impossible, barring the death of Lyndon Johnson or, equally unlikely, a decision by Johnson not to seek a second full term. (Bobby

(opposite page, top) Portrait of a leading American politician, aided by daughter Kathleen, about to take the plunge. (bottom) Bob Kennedy greets his wife after her rescue from the rapids of the Hudson river. Ethel's kayak tipped her over three times into the freezing water. The temperature was in the forties — with snow flurries.

must fear, whether he will admit it or not, the possibility that Lyndon Johnson could die in office, elevating Humphrey to the Presidency, crushing or at least postponing the Kennedy plans.) Bobby knows that his best chance to win the nomination appears to be in 1972, but he knows, too, that Johnson could lose in 1968, that a Republican could capture the White House for eight years, that the 1972 nomination could be worthless.

Kennedy knows all the factors working against him, and still his target remains the Presidency, "the place," he once said, "to do most to get things done." The secondary choices do not tempt him. Larry O'Brien has suggested that Kennedy could become a decisive voice in the Senate, but Bobby has little passion for the Senate. He could turn to teaching, or to publishing a newspaper or a magazine, but the lure of politics, the desire for power, appears too strong. Perhaps even if his brother had not been assassinated, Bobby Kennedy would, eventually, have bid for the Presidency.

He is driven now by a curious mixture of fatalism and impatience. He admits he cannot hurry the political timetable. He knows that in 1976, he will be only fifty, younger than most Presidents at the time of their election, and that in 1984, if the world survives to the Orwellian year, he will be fifty-eight, hardly ancient by Presidential standards. But even as he concedes the futility of pressing too hard too soon for the Presidency, he keeps looking for the proper moment. He seems to suspect that his popularity will rise again, possibly for reasons beyond logic, and when and if he finds the proper moment, he will act.

The Kennedy money is ready, enormous sums, and no one can overestimate the importance of money in a Presidential campaign today. The Kennedy machine is ready too. A man like Ed Guthman, far from Washington in his Los Angeles newspaper job, insists he cannot await the birth of a new Kennedy dynasty. "In 1972," Guthman says, "I'll be fifty-two." But if the call should come for aid in a Presidential campaign, Guthman almost certainly would respond; so would Pierre Salinger in California, John Seigenthaler in Nashville, Ted Sorensen in New York, the men at Harvard and in Washington who form the heart of the amorphous Kennedy party, the ministers in the vague shadow cabinet. No real cabinet exists—"unless," says John Kenneth Galbraith, "this cabinet is a thing of such singular originality that it never meets and never discusses anything"—but the men are available.

The Presidency can never be far from Bobby Kennedy's mind; no man in his position could completely submerge the notion. But he stubbornly refuses to look far ahead. Of 1972, he says, "Who knows whether any of us will still be alive then? Existence is so fickle, fate is so fickle."

"Kennedy refuses to abandon his youthful, long-haired image, which irritates many voters." Runs in the family.

R. F. K.

The Kennedy family's 1964
Christmas card. Left to right:
David, Joe, Kerry (holding
rabbit), Kathleen, Christopher,
Bobby (holding chicken),
Michael (holding bird), and
Courtney.

JOE   BOBBY   KATHLEEN   MATTHEW

His fatalism is as real as his desire to be President. One evening in 1967, Kennedy sat in his plane, *The Caroline*, a full day's tour behind him, a bourbon-and-ice in front of him, his sleeves rolled up, and he considered, briefly, his future. "Right now," he said, "as a senator, I'm dealing only with my own personal future. It's not so important."

A reporter expressed surprise that Kennedy could view his own life so lightly. "Oh, it's important," Bobby conceded, "but it's not as important as it was, as it used to be."

"Do you think you could ever work for anybody else again?" he was asked.

Bobby hesitated. "Other than the person I worked for?" he said.

The reporter nodded. "No," said Bobby. "No. I don't think so."

His eyes glazed momentarily, the way they often do, and perhaps he thought fleetingly of the power days in Washington, the days when he and his brother

The Kennedys' 1965 Christmas card.

DAVID   KERRY   MICHAEL   COURTNEY
                                             CHRISTOPHER

believed they could alter, if only slightly, the course of history. "We were all involved in certain tasks, in certain dreams," he once said.

His dream persists, the dream of another Kennedy in the White House, but Bobby Kennedy understands, perhaps better than his friends and his enemies, the distance between dream and reality. In the spring of 1967, a college student questioned him about the frightening word-picture Gore Vidal had recently painted of an endless Kennedy dynasty.

"Gore who?" said Bobby Kennedy.

He paused, enjoying the laughter he had provoked. "I would say," he added, "that the chances for a Kennedy dynasty are looking very slim."

R. F. K.

R. F. K.

He smiled as he spoke, and the words were light, but the reasoning behind them seemed valid. Powered by complex impulses, engulfed by angry enemies, a man of controversy and not of consensus, Robert Francis Kennedy must be rated only a contender, not a favorite, to become President of the United States.

His own assessment rings true. The idea of a Kennedy dynasty does seem remote.

And, only a decade ago, the idea of a forty-three-year-old Catholic becoming President of the United States seemed ridiculous.

The tree house at Hickory Hill.

"Kennedy recognizes the erratic nature of political popularity. He is no more depressed
by his sagging showings in the polls of 1967 than he is elated by the posters blaring,
'Bobby in '68.' 'Bobby in '72,' 'Bobby Anytime,' or by the unauthorized committees
boosting him for President in 1968 . . . His fatalism is as real as his desire to be President."

ABOUT THE AUTHOR

Dick Schaap was senior editor of *Newsweek* at the age of twenty-seven, city editor of the New York *Herald Tribune* at twenty-nine, and a syndicated columnist at thirty. Born in Brooklyn and educated at Cornell and Columbia universities, he started his professional career as a sportswriter, contributed more than one hundred free-lance articles to national magazines, wrote biographies of Mickey Mantle and Paul Hornung and *An Illustrated History of the Olympics.* A frequent lecturer, occasional television commentator, and member of the faculty of Columbia's Graduate School of Journalism, his work has appeared in a dozen anthologies. His recent book, *Turned On: The Friede-Crenshaw Case*, was a study of narcotics addiction.

ABOUT THE PICTURE EDITOR

Michael O'Keefe is a picture editor on the Sunday staff of *The New York Times.* He joined the paper in 1941, left for three years of Army service in World War II, returning in 1946.

He has been a picture editor and consultant on a number of books involving domestic and world affairs, among them *The Kennedy Years*; *The Truman Presidency* by Cabell Phillips; and *The Road To The White House*, the story of the 1964 Presidential campaign. He was also co-editor of a four-volume text and picture history of World War II.

A resident of New Jersey, where he was born and educated, he lives in Rutherford, with his wife and three children.

PICTURE CREDITS